Do What You Do Better™ for Salespeople

Marc A. Corsini

Corsini's Do What You Do Better Publishing
Birmingham, Alabama

Corsini's Do What You Do Better Publishing
6 Office Park Circle, Suite 309
Birmingham, AL 35223-2542
(205) 879-0432
marc@corsini.com
www.corsini.com

First Printing August 2008

ISBN-13 978-0-9791572-3-3
ISBN-10 0-9791572-3-4

Publisher: Marc A. Corsini
Design and Production: Chuck Watkins
Editor: Susan Swagler

Printed in the United States of America

Acknowledgements

My first year out of college, I was blessed to discover where my passion and my talents intersected—in selling.

For almost 30 years, I have been involved in the sales process in one way or another. I started, like most people in this career, as a young and inexperienced salesperson. Then I advanced to become a sales manager for a major corporation. And now, for almost 20 years, I have been a sales and executive coach—helping others nurture their own passion and hone their own talents for sales.

Along the way, I never stopped learning. I remember that first summer, as a brand-new, green-as-grass salesperson, driving in my car in my territory while listening to every sales and business book on tape I could find at the local library. I wanted to know everything about how to be a rainmaker. I still do. First, of course, I wanted that knowledge for myself; now I'm committed to sharing what I've learned so I can help other companies do what they do better by developing their people to be rainmakers and their executives to be leaders.

This book is dedicated to all of the many salespeople we have coached at Corsini Consulting Group, LLC who have shown us exactly what it takes to be a true rainmaker. Rainmakers are not born; they become the best through a tremendous desire to achieve, focused discipline and an unwavering commitment toward success each and every day. Coaching this elite group of salespeople and seeing them perfect their craft day after day, month after month, year after year, continues to be a privilege and an honor.

Just as I've helped these people, I've also had some assistance along the way. I'd like to thank Susan Swagler who helped with all aspects of this book. Her insights, comments and editorial wordsmithing were a tremendous help to me.

And finally, I'd like to thank Susan, my wife, who supports and encourages me in all that I do. She is my rock, and I love her with all of my heart. I never really understood *true* success until she came into my life.

Foreword

The purpose of this book, much like my first book, is pretty straightforward: to help businesspeople do what they do better—both in and out of their offices. The real difference with this book is in the focus. It is specifically and decidedly written for salespeople who want a better understanding of selling and the sales process. This is for those select salespeople who have a burning desire to be a rainmaker.

In some ways this book is a "how-to" for salespeople who are driven to succeed. But that's not the only reason for writing it. Certainly inside these pages, you'll find a proven game plan for success and plenty of strategic how-tos to help you become a true rainmaker. But there's more here. Much, much more. That's because we're looking at a larger picture. *Do What You Do Better for Salespeople* also addresses "how to" achieve success in *all* areas of your life—not just professionally. This is how you realize *true* success. This kind of success extends far beyond the office and what happens there. It impacts *all* areas of your life. This is the all-encompassing success you've always wanted.

My first book outlined the principles of **The 7 F's of *True* Success**. I introduced readers to the seven components of a truly and fully successful life: the **Fundamentals** of work, **Finances** (and your financial legacy), **Family** (and friends), **Faith**, **Fitness** (emotional and physical), **Fun** and the **Fusion** (or balance) of all these things. This model works beautifully. So we will continue to follow it in this book.

Hole vs. Whole

We've all known highly successful salespeople. Those people who appear to have their goals well in hand and every deal going their way. They're probably setting records and examples to follow in their chosen professions. They might be seen as the biggest rainmakers in their fields. Heck, they might even be legendary in their lines of work. But things aren't always as they seem. Sometimes, if you pull back the curtain on some of these lives, you'll see that success—no matter how impressive—doesn't extend to life outside the office. There are "holes" everywhere. In some cases, their personal lives are in shambles.

That isn't the case with a "whole-life" approach to success. In our sales coaching model, we coach you to discover the rainmaker within you. And we do everything we can to help you focus on the prize and realize your goals. But, at the same time, we help you define and *achieve* a real and workable balance in your life. And then, through accountability and concentrated effort, we help you keep it. This is how you achieve *true* success—we're talking about success in *all* areas of your life. In short, our coaching methods take a "whole life" approach to your success that helps you avoid the holes.

This isn't a larger-than-life idea. Rather, it's a large-as-life method. And that makes it worth pursuing.

One Book, Two Parts

This book is divided into two main parts. In the first half, we focus on the **Fundamentals of Work** for you as a salesperson. Essentially, these are the **Fundamentals of Selling,** and they are your "how-tos" for being a rainmaker. We explore and emphasize the importance of being an advisor to your clients and new relationships. We talk about how to overachieve in sales using the abundance principle and our Best Bets™ Model of focusing on a select group of new opportunities.

The "how-to" concept continues with a host of proven sales tips. Next, we offer some workable ideas for winning presentations. We give you tools to implement an effective referral system so you'll always have an ongoing source of new opportunities. We offer you a fresh, new way to negotiate so that everyone comes away a winner. And we offer ways to be as productive as you can *without* working 70 to 80 hours each week.

Once you have the **Fundamentals** in hand, we move on to the second part of the book, which is devoted to those areas of your life outside the office. We discuss the rich and lasting legacy you can leave for your family (and your family's family) by taking control of your **Finances** (and creating your financial legacy). We talk about how to turn your attention to **Family** (and friends) and keep your commitments to them. Next, we discuss how to make your **Faith** a daily and meaningful part of your life—not just a once-a-week-for-an-hour activity.

We know that the sales profession is stressful and emotionally challenging, so we talk about how **Fitness** plays an effective role in keeping you mentally and physically healthy (and at the top of your game). A healthy lifestyle is a happy lifestyle. And with that in mind, we focus on the importance of having enough **Fun** in your life. In addition to being part of a whole-life approach to, well, life, we believe you should find joy in your work. You gotta love what you do, and you have to have fun doing it.

Then, the balance comes from bringing all this together. **Fusion** is the happy and fulfilling culmination of your work in all of these aspects of your life. When you find success in each of these areas—the **Fundamentals of Selling**, **Finances** (and creating your financial legacy)**, Family** (and friends), **Faith**, **Fitness** (emotional and physical) and **Fun**, you'll find *true* success. **Fusion** is the tricky part. Most people can find success in one or two areas of their lives, but when you make it your goal to have it all, that takes focus, determination and hard work. We'll show you how to do that and keep up the good work.

The Corsini Challenge

What you hold in your hands holds the key to a more successful life. But all the how-tos in the world won't make that happen unless you take charge. I am challenging you to be authentic with yourself and strive to fully embrace this book—applying the concepts we present to *all* areas of your life. Each and every one. At CCG, we've coached countless people who, at first, were skeptical of this whole-life approach. But after making our methods their own, they've realized the real meaning of *true* success. And now they are reaping the rewards.

Here's something else I know: You can do this, too. You'll be thankful you did. And along the way you will Do What You Do Better!

Table Of Contents

The Fundamentals of Work for Salespeople

"Basic, day-to-day work fundamentals, if replicated well and intentionally, always produce results."

— Marc Corsini

INSIDE

Fundamental to Success in Sales

We believe to be successful in anything in life, you have to master the fundamentals of whatever it is that you are trying to achieve. Professional athletes (even, or perhaps especially, the champions) spend their entire careers focusing on the basics. Golfers, no matter how many matches they win, still get coaches to help enhance their game. Baseball has spring training—every spring. Football players work every off-season with trainers on strength, flexibility, skill and speed.

Salespeople who overachieve in their profession year after year are committed to the same philosophy of continuously honing their techniques, getting more experience and growing their business. They are always working on their sales skills, product knowledge, presentation abilities, time-management techniques, negotiation smarts, knowledge of industry trends, expansion of their centers of influence, etc.

In this chapter, we offer some of what we view as the essential ingredients to being a rainmaker. Our sales coaching experience has proven, year after year, that if a salesperson truly focuses on their **Fundamentals of Selling**, they become the rainmaker they are capable of being.

By no means do we believe our list is all-inclusive. We fully understand that when someone achieves "rainmaker status," they have done so by doing 1,000 different things in order to be successful. There can never be one specific activity that makes someone a rainmaker, but there are several core fundamentals to the sales process that are essential to success—no matter what you're selling.

In the coming pages, we offer a few of the fundamentals we use to help some of the top rainmakers in the country Do What They Do Better.

Fundamental to Success in Sales

What are the basic activities that make you successful? The chances are, whatever you list will fall somewhere within the fundamentals we're about to discuss. Figure out what's fundamental to your success, and then commit to doing those things—and doing them well—consistently. You know what works for you. We know what has worked well for hundreds of others. Put it all together, and you'll do what you do better.

Life-Long Commitment to Doing What You Do Better

Probably the most important core trait shared by all rainmakers is a life-long commitment to doing what they do better. To be the best, year after year, you have to continuously learn about your industry, hone your craft and focus on just about every aspect of the sales profession.

That includes increasing your sales and product knowledge, perfecting your negotiation and presentation skills, learning to better use technology, understanding industry trends, managing your time, balancing your personal and professional lives and being organized. Just to name a few things! You need to be current and competitive on multiple fronts. And in the long run, you should do this effortlessly and effectively. Your goal is to be viewed as an expert in your field. A "go-to" person. A leader in your profession.

Bottom line: You want to set yourself apart from the norm and essentially be in a class all your own. Yes, this is setting the bar quite high. And, yes, you can do it—if you make a life-long commitment to doing what you do better.

Adapting the Advisory Sales Model

Once upon a time, lots of good will coupled with sufficient product knowledge and some effective sales ability were the basic ingredients of a successful sales process. This was all you needed for a sound sales relationship. But not anymore.

Companies today want more. Much, much more. They demand more from their salespeople because their business is becoming increasingly more sophisticated. Clients today want partners and advisors to help them in their business.

If you want to be truly successful long-term, you have to give the clients what they want—even if they sometimes don't know what they want or need. That's why it takes an advisory approach to sales in order to be successful today. That means taking on an active role in your client's success.

You have to ask meaningful questions and then actively listen to their answers. You need to go in and observe your client's business, really understand it and then ask more questions. You should meet with people in the organization (other than your contact) and ask them questions. Then, and only then, and always in an advisory role, do you come up with a recommendation or a solution to their needs.

Why are we so passionate about salespeople becoming advisors? Simply this: Companies are no longer willing to pay a premium just for a product. Products alone are perceived as commodities—and commodities are sold on price. And if you are in the "price game," then you must realize that low price wins the game. You will not always have the lowest price. But if you truly understand your client's business, if you are an advisor to your client rather than just a supplier of goods or services, you'll have something more to offer. Something your competition might not have.

Besides, if you do your job as an advisor effectively, you'll work smarter not necessarily harder. You'll know if there is an opportunity there for you or not. As an advisor, you have intimate knowledge of your client's business. You have an ongoing dialogue, and you'll know when opportunity presents itself. Just as you'll know if the time or situation is not right for what you're offering. Your job as an advisor is not to simply sell someone something, it is to determine if and when and how you can best address your client's needs.

Today, if you want to keep clients and attract new opportunities, you have to provide advice and be a consultant to your clients. You have to exceed their expectations.

Abundant Best Bets™ Opportunities Pipeline

You should have a full inventory of opportunities at all times. But not all opportunities are created equal. The Corsini Best Bets™ Model encourages salespeople to focus on a *limited, manageable, smart* number of opportunities. Oftentimes the number of current and future opportunities totals 30, 60 or, in many cases, up to 120. That's reasonable. Nobody can focus on 1,200 names in a database. No one can be an advisor to 1,000 companies. But a rainmaker *can* be an advisor to 30 or 60 or 120 companies over the next one, three or five years.

Many salespeople have 1,200 (or more!) names in their contact management systems. Of that list, 5 percent might be your Best Bets™ Pipeline opportunities. If you follow our model every day and adapt our abundance principle (which recognizes that opportunities are everywhere), you will maintain a full inventory of opportunities at all times.

"Touch" Programs

"Touches" are activities you do regarding your Best Bets™ Opportunities in order to keep your name in front of them. Sometimes this is called a "drip marketing program." Whatever you call it, you should be following some procedure and performing some activity consistently to keep your name "top of mind" with current clients as well as new opportunities. This way, they know who you are and, more importantly, you are easily recalled when they have a problem or opportunity you can address. Touch programs include emails, phone calls, faxes, newsletters, articles, seminars, entertainment, birthday and holiday cards, personal notes, etc. Whatever you do, you want your touch program to focus on your name; what you offer; and, most critically, how you can help them as an advisor in their business.

If possible, delegate or outsource your touch program as much as possible so you can focus on actually meeting with, talking to and communicating with your clients and your targeted Best Bets™ Opportunities. Remember: You focus your time and talents on being a trusted advisor to your clients and new relationships, and your staff, where applicable, supports and implements your "touch" programs.

High Activity

The fuel that drives the sales engine is activity. Activity includes all the things that you do with clients and new relationships to first get on their radar and then demonstrate you are an advisor to them. The cornerstone of a successful sales career involves taking care of your clients. If they are not satisfied, you are simply "renting" clients for the short term.

This takes work.

We believe you should spend most of your time in front of and talking to your clients and new relationships. To understand their business, you have to spend time *at* their business. To understand their challenges and opportunities, you have to spend time *with* them. With the salespeople in our program, we track the number of face-to-face visits with their Best Bets™ Opportunities and new relationships they might want in their pipeline in the future. We do this not as "police work," but as one of the indicators of success.

Most salespeople find it relatively easy to focus on and give attention to their existing clients—the weak spot for a lot of salespeople is in the area of developing new relationships. Our model emphasizes the importance of regularly adding additional clients through new opportunities. Remember, it's not *if* you lose that big client one day, but *when* you lose that client. You develop new relationships through spending time with them and working hard to understand their business.

We emphasize high activity, not just "for the numbers." High activity is how you keep your clients happy. It's how you develop meaningful relationships. It's how you become an advisor. Work hard, keep your activity high (with current and new clients), and the success will follow.

Ongoing Game Experience

High activity keeps you busy in many ways. If you use the advisory sales model correctly, keep up the touches and do it consistently, you'll encounter new opportunities often and enjoy profitable game experience all year round. High activity leads to meaningful relationships; meaningful relationships lead to an advisory role; being an advisor to your clients leads to new opportunities with new and existing clients.

If you spend your time wisely, you'll be spending the majority of it with clients. New relationships and new opportunities come from this focused effort. Proposals and recommendations result. From recommendations, you gain game experiences of wins and losses. That's fine. Both help you grow in different ways. Rainmakers get regular game experience by closing new opportunities year round. Their game experience (wins and loses) is ongoing.

Referrals

We know of no better way to grow your book of business than through referrals. Cold calling is the long, hard way. Use your centers of influence (your CPA, attorney, colleagues, social connections, etc.) to generate referrals. Current, satisfied clients are an excellent source of referrals that can lead directly to new, profitable relationships. These focused, strategic calls are much easier (and have a much higher payoff) than cold calling. Experienced salespeople should generate the bulk of their new opportunities through referrals and their high-activity touch programs. Make sure you are asking for referrals and following up on them on a regular basis.

We challenge you to ask for and get a minimum of two referrals per month. Follow up on each referral, and then send a thank-you note to the referral source.

We believe so strongly in this fundamental that we have devoted an entire chapter to it. Look to Reference Points for more information.

Authenticity in Everything You Do

Have you ever heard this joke?

> Question: "How can you tell if a salesperson is lying?"

> Answer: "Their lips are moving."

It's really not that funny, and we'd like for it *never* to be true. To really be the best of the best, you have to be authentic in everything you do. No lies, no half-truths and no cover-ups. Ever. This is absolutely essential if you are to be a trusted advisor to your clients.

Being authentic is tough. Sometimes in the short term "white lies" and half-truths might be easier than being upfront and perfectly honest. But in the long haul, there is no substitute for authenticity. None!

Be Present in the Moment

When dealing with people in the sales process, you have to be present in the moment. You can't be thinking about your kid's baseball game that afternoon, the cracked window at home, the administrative emergency at the office, the 150 emails in your inbox, or the countless other distractions and to-dos that you have going on in your life.

Nope. You have to be 100 percent focused on the person you are meeting with or talking to on the phone. You have to ask meaningful questions. These questions should be logical in their order. Then you have to actively listen to what they are (and are not) saying. To hear what they are *not* saying requires a total commitment to hearing, seeing and feeling what they *are* saying.

During your time together, you should be saying things like:

- "Tell me more…"
- "What did you mean when you said…?"
- "How did what you just said impact your business…?"
- "Let me make sure I understand what you want…"

Give the client your undivided attention. Always.

Value-Add

Selling on price is an old and tired strategy. It doesn't take any sophistication and savvy to sell on price. And, what's more, it will only get you so far. Then what?

Trying to be the lost-cost provider in anything is hard—damn hard. And if you are competing on price, you are telling the buyer your product is a commodity. Plain and simple. Nothing more, nothing less. In the commodity game, low price wins.

So in today's competitive environment with sophisticated buyers, you have to step up to the plate and offer more than just a good price. You have to provide more than what is expected in the normal sales relationship. These are things that you and your company do that are above and beyond what the product promises and what the competition provides.

You have to figure out how you are *differentiating* yourself from others. Look at what you and your company can do in addition to helping your clients with the product or service you offer and they need. Value-add takes the form of professional services others are not providing such as faster shipping, financing alternatives, reducing your clients' risks, saving them time, offering them advice, bringing in other resources, providing your clients with the latest software, etc. Bottom line: Do more than the client expects and more than the competition is offering.

Remember, there are lots of places to go for good products and services. Make the sales experience with you different in as many good ways as possible.

Planning

Working without a plan is like hunting in the dark. You might shoot a lot—but will you hit anything? Planning is an ongoing activity. Each year, develop your 12-month strategic sales plan. Update it quarterly. Then make sure to review it monthly.

Your **strategic sales plan** should include your sales and professional development goals. Devote a section to an assessment of your current book of business. Document your existing client and new relationship opportunities. Include your centers of influence. Plan how you are going to further develop current relationships and identify new sources that might be mutually beneficial.

Make weekly time in your schedule to plan and measure your progress. Strive to spend at least one hour each week simply planning your strategy. You'll have plenty of time in the rest of the week to execute these plans. And you'll work smarter.

Add Your Own

We challenge you to come up with your own **Fundamentals of Selling**. Most companies we work with have their own fundamentals based on their culture, their geography, their industry, etc.

Whether your company's fundamentals are spelled out or not, it's important to figure out what works best for you in your situation.

Time for the Other F's

One of the most important **Fundamentals of Selling** for a truly successful salesperson involves making time for the other F's in your life—**Finances** (and your financial legacy), **Family** (and friends), **Faith, Fitness, Fun** and the **Fusion,** or balance, of all these things. All work and no play Is no fun for anyone. Make time for life outside the office. Pay attention to these other F's. Schedule time for them just as you do for client-related activities. This is key to a successful, happy, balanced life. This is how you achieve *true* success.

Be Creative

Add to what we've offered you. Our fundamentals cover a lot of ground. Yours are specific to your situation. Put together, they all will help you Do What You Do Better.

Corsini's Best Bets™ Model

"Follow our Best Bets™ Model,
and I promise that you will Do What You Do Better."
— Marc Corsini

INSIDE
The Sales Profession: A Historical Perspective
Corsini's Best Bets™ Model
Sales Stages of the Best Bets™ Opportunities Pipeline

Selling is never static.

The job of the sales professional continues to evolve, and, as it changes, it becomes more and more complex. It has to, though, because business is becoming more complicated and clients increasingly are more sophisticated.

In order to know where we're going, sometimes it helps to first see where we've been. To that end, let's take a look at how selling has changed over the decades. Then we'll see how **Corsini's Best Bets™ Model** helps you achieve success today and overachieve in the future.

At one time, a hearty handshake and a fancy dinner led to landing the account. Not anymore. It takes more than entertainment to build a book of business. Companies today want more than just an invitation to the holiday party. Much, much more. **These days, clients want partners in their success. They demand straight talk. They need knowledgeable advisors to help them in their business.** So what's a great salesperson to do?

Well, **less**, for starters.

Oftentimes, a salesperson lacks focus and a workable, strategic sales plan. They have too many names in the database; too many distractions; and not enough time, energy or resources to establish which possible clients will be the most profitable.

Corsini's Best Bets™ Model illustrates that more is not better. **In fact, *less* is more—in terms of allowing you to focus your time, talents and treasures on select opportunities.** We'll show you how to determine which of your current clients and prospective opportunities are the most profitable to you. And along the way, you'll do what you do better—achieving professional success and allowing precious time for the balance you want in your life.

Our sales model is based on **four crucial components**, which are fundamentally important to any rainmaker's success. These components are:

- adapting an **advisory approach** to the sales process;
- developing a **strategic sales plan** for a select group of clients and new relationship opportunities that we call the **Best Bets™ Opportunities Pipeline**;
- maintaining a **year-round high level of activity**; and
- developing and implementing an **ongoing accountability** program.

We developed this process-based model over the past 20 years. It is designed to help you determine your focus during the next 3, 12 and 18 months. By following our **Best Bets™ Model** you will get a workable game plan showing you how and where you should spend your time and resources in order to more effectively Do What You Do Better.

The Sales Profession:
A Historical Perspective

Before we look forward, let's glance back at a short history of modern selling.

The skills required of the sales professional have changed drastically over the past 50 years. This change is a direct reflection of the increased complexity of the business environment and what is required of a salesperson today.

In the 1950s, salespeople had to primarily know their products well and possess some sales skills. Entertaining was a big part of the sales process. The job wasn't easy, but neither was it complex.

Selling for big companies was the ticket back then. A 1949 survey in *Fortune* found that the typical college graduate then wanted *"to work for somebody else—preferably someone big."* This was a generation that believed *"big brother will take care of you."*

The tools required to do the sales job in the 1950s were the telephone, an automobile, a briefcase, product brochures, an expense account and the ability to close an opportunity.

Back then, the client relied heavily on the salesperson's product knowledge and expertise because that salesperson knew more about the product or service than did the client. This relationship—while mostly mutually beneficial—was nonetheless controlled by the salesperson. And there wasn't a lot of competition. ***"Trust me; we'll take care of you,"*** was the credo of the day. The buyers often were entertained to keep them happy.

The 1960s started the "marketing revolution." With the increasing popularity of television and other immediate medias, **the salesperson's product and sales expertise usually was complemented by some type of marketing campaign.** In small-to medium-sized companies, salespeople had to understand, develop and sometimes know how to implement their own marketing programs. And commercial jet service made long-distance sales trips much more affordable and timesaving.

In the 1970s, business calls became a fast, flip-through exercise for millions of salespeople who relied on the Rolodex. This period brought not only a marked cultural change, but also a change in selling habits. Buyers were becoming more sophisticated. They wanted more than product samples and cocktails. **Increased competition shifted the focus to service**.

Beginning in the 1980s, the salesperson's "toolbox" became even more technical. Word processors improved the quality of sales and marketing communications. What's more, salespeople quickly started using computers to communicate their messages to the masses. Of course, technology has developed and expanded exponentially over the past 20 years. As a result, the focus for many salespeople has gotten bigger because, with increased and improved technology, they can cover more ground in less time.

And, increasingly, clients started wanting even more. **Service wasn't enough; they wanted *solutions*.** Buyers were saying: *"Don't just sell me something. Tell me how I can use it to increase revenues or improve my bottom line."* The effective salesperson responded with answers. For instance, in the computer industry, this often meant that a computer company had to team with a software firm in order to provide a packaged solution.

In the past decade, technology for salespeople has skyrocketed. Everything from Web-based contact-managers to digital phones to automated presentations and the Internet help the salesperson be more productive and efficient. But this productivity is not without a price: Now, not only do salespeople have to sell (and do it quickly), but they also **have to have average (or above average) technology skills**.

What this boils down to today is this: The minimum base line to do the sales job requires that you have product knowledge, business smarts, industry expertise, sales ability and technology skills just to survive. And that is *only* just to survive. Clients today demand even more—especially if you want to be a rainmaker year after year.

The final and most important skill needed to excel at selling today is the ability to be an advisor to your clients. The first component of our Best Bets ™ Model is an advisory sales approach. It's about asking questions, encouraging open dialogue, interpreting what clients need (even if they don't know what they need) and then providing them with the kind of advice to help them do what they do better.

If you want to be truly successful at sales long-term, you have to give the clients what they want. And today's clients want advice not just appetizers. They are looking for, expecting—and yes, even demanding—a partner in their success. Companies need more from salespeople because their business is becoming more and more sophisticated. Today's clients usually are armed with enough knowledge, experience and expertise to get what they want, when they want it and on their terms. That's why it takes an advisory approach—the value-add that tips the scales in your favor—to be successful at selling. This takes a lot of work, focus and dedication on your part. You have to listen, question, probe, assess, ask more questions, meet with others in the company, listen some more and then provide a solution that is tailored to your clients' needs.

With technology becoming more commonplace, the Internet allows anyone to become a savvy buyer with a simple click of the mouse. **What clients want today is a knowledgeable, trusted advisor to help them sort through their multitude of choices and grow their overall business.** They want to know how to increase productivity, improve revenue, reduce risks and limit their costs. **Rainmakers don't just talk products and promises—they deliver advice and answers.**

Companies are no longer willing to pay a premium just for a product. Products alone are simply commodities, and commodities are sold on price. Low price wins this game, and you can't always have the lowest price.

Providing additional value gives you the edge. And, indeed, it has become the mantra for successful sales organizations. Forward-thinking salespeople are constantly trying to look for opportunities to provide additional value and then to justify their "value-added" service to clients. Where they are successful, the client pays a premium. Where the value-add cannot be justified, the client balks at paying a premium and goes back to the price game. When this happens, discounting comes into play.

Where your client perceives you on their mental "pricing options chart" determines the price they are willing to pay for your services. The buyer ultimately decides where you are in the price chart. **It is your job as a salesperson to justify your place there.**

Today's fast-paced, technologically advanced workplace works in your favor. With increased competition, sophistication of buyers in the marketplace, easy access to information and time demands of life in and out of the office for both the buyer and the seller, your value-add can do a lot to make the buyer's life (and job) easier. But you have to absolutely and authentically buy in to your clients' success. **Today, if you want to keep clients and attract new opportunities, you have to be a *partner* in your clients' success**.

Corsini's
Best Bets™ Model

This idea of partnering in your clients' success is so important that we put it first in our **Best Bets™ Model**. Here's why it is so essential to our method: When you become a partner in your clients' success, you operate in an atmosphere of trust where your work is fulfilling and promising and new opportunities come your way as a matter of course. People like to do business with people they trust. And they like to recommend these trusted advisors to others. One thing leads to another, and you're working in a way that is not as much "work" as you would think.

That said, let's look carefully at the four vital components of the **Best Bets™ Model**. They are:

- adapting an **advisory approach** to the sales process;
- developing a **strategic sales plan** for a select group of clients and new relationship opportunities that we call the **Best Bets™ Opportunities Pipeline**;

- maintaining a **year-round high level of activity**; and
- developing and implementing an **ongoing accountability** program.

Once you decide to become a real part of your clients' success, you'll need to approach their business (and the way you do business) with a strategic sales plan. You'll need to maintain a high level of activity all the time—even when you have all the work you can handle. And an ongoing accountability program will keep you on track. This is a proven way to Do What You Do Better.

An Advisory Approach to the Sales Process

How much is too much?

Over the past decade, technology advancements and communications changes have allowed salespeople to capture names and company information easily and quickly. The result? The average salesperson has more contacts than he or she could possibly take care of in a year (or two or three).

In the past, this was considered a good thing. "More was better." The famous (or infamous) "sales funnel" advocated handling as many clients and prospects as you could. The idea was that by reaching more people, you could make more money.

The result of this? Salespeople are apt to lose focus in the face of all the "stuff," and they become overwhelmed in the minutiae of emails, faxes, voice mails, too many non-productive meetings, etc. In the very worst case, the salesperson's focus (such as it is) shifts entirely from the client to internal-related issues.

Our approach is different. We coach that more isn't necessarily better—it's just more. And more means more (unnecessary) work.

In our experience, the successful, practiced rainmaker ignores the funnel mentality (i.e. the bigger the funnel, the better) and instead **focuses on a few, select clients and prospective new opportunities.** It's a way to work smarter, not necessarily harder. And this model allows you the freedom and opportunity to be an advisor.

Dan Sullivan coined the phrase, "the ceiling of complexity." **This is the point where the salesperson is out of control and weighed down with the details of servicing existing clients, handling problems and trying to do an occasional prospecting call.** Let's face it: Selling is not simple. You have to know your product inside and out, you have to be an effective salesperson, you need to know everything there is to know about your industry, you have to take care of current clients and find new ones and you have to be up-to-date on the latest technology. At the same time, we're challenging you to take an advisory role with your clients. So it's imperative that you work efficiently and effectively. There's just no other way to do it.

Another reason to embrace our advisory role to selling is because the typical salesperson-client relationship has become dysfunctional—especially in a new business/new relationship role. Popular sales negotiating books tell us "information is king." It's also easy to come by—especially with the Internet. An advisory role grows in an atmosphere of trust, and that's where you want to be. Without that sense of trust, clients feel that if they give out too much information in a selling situation, then the salesperson later uses that information against them.

At the same time, thanks to mass media, clients (and salespeople) are able to gather more information on their own. That's a lot of information floating around but not much real sharing. When this happens, clients often leave sales meetings feeling the salesperson is doing something "to" them—not "for" or "with" them. The salesperson leaves frustrated that he or she can only go so far with the client. Bottom line: The walls go up, the dialogue is minimized (or stops altogether) and both parties lose. This doesn't happen in a situation built on trust and mutual admiration.

Being an advisor to your client *requires* **you to be outwardly focused.** As we mentioned earlier, technology is a double-edged sword for today's salesperson. For those who use it wisely, it is a priceless productivity tool—improving communications, streamlining time management, and managing clients and new opportunities. For so many others, however, technology has become the job. This is what happens when you waste valuable time on non-sales related phone calls, getting and reading emails, checking voice mail and surfing the Web. You become inwardly focused instead of focusing on your clients' success and your hand in it.

And so we coach that less is more. Simple is in. We tell our salespeople: Focus on the few so you can take an authentic advisory approach to the sales process. But how do you know whom to focus on?

Working With a Strategic Sales Plan

The first component of our **Best Bets™ Model** challenges the salesperson to **be an advisor to clients and new relationships.** The second part of the model has salespeople **developing their strategic sales plan** for a select group of their current clients and new relationship opportunities using our **Best Bets™ Opportunities Pipeline.** This idea is based, in part, on the 80/20 Principle.

The 80/20 Principle is a great application for salespeople. We didn't discover it, but we (and hundreds of people who've used our programs) have embraced it and applied it with fantastic results to today's hectic pace.

According to the 80/20 Principle, **80 percent of the results, outputs or rewards are derived from only 20 percent of the causes, inputs or efforts.**

By applying this to your own time and productivity, you can **determine where you should spend 80 percent of your time.** As we examine the client base of our top rainmakers, our research continually shows that if they have 100 clients, a minimum of 80 percent of their business comes from only 20 percent of these clients. **So, why should anyone focus their sales and marketing efforts on all 100 clients when only 10 to 20 of the clients are providing the majority of their revenue and profit?** No good reason, except that we have a hard time getting away from the idea that "more is better," and that we should treat every client and all new opportunities the same.

The fact that they are not the same is precisely why we developed the **Best Bets™ Opportunities Pipeline.** Our model applies the 80/20 Principle to opportunities and salespeople. And I have a simple theory as to why it works.

First, let's look at how new companies and a lot of new sales positions are established. **Most companies start when one or more salespeople leave one company to start a new company. Or in some cases, a salesperson moves to a competitor and starts over—usually with some of their former clients.** Think about it. New insurance agencies often are created when one or more producers leave their agencies and take with them any and all of the clients that will move. The same thing usually happens when a producer leaves one agency to take a different job with another agency.

If the producer has 100 clients and 20 are the "best" in terms of revenue generated, when they leave one company to go with another firm they will normally take about 10 of the high-revenue clients with them. The rest left behind are those who won't agree to move. Then, of the 80 or so remaining clients in their book of business, the producer might get 20 or more of them to come along. So the producer starts the new job with 30 to 40 clients and quickly gets to work building a new book of business.

Using the "I gotta build back my book of business quickly" strategy, the producer, now at a new company, focuses on, and then adds to their book of business, anyone who is willing to talk to them and be receptive to their sales efforts. In many cases, these most likely are average to poor opportunities (in terms of revenue potential) from some other producer's book of business. Over a period of time, the producer will pick up another 40 to 50 clients, mostly providing average revenue potential along with an occasional high-revenue client added in the mix.

Without the focus of enough solid opportunities, the producer builds a book of business with anyone who will talk to them, resulting in a lot of average clients with little big opportunity for the future. In the end, the salesperson is back where they started—with a book of business that contains about 100 clients and of that 100 only 10 to 20 are their "best" in terms of revenue generated. And so the dysfunctional cycle continues.

We have developed a Best Bets™ Pipeline Model in which salespeople focus on only a small number of clients and new opportunities during a 12- to 18-month process; and they do this using the advisory sales approach. This model is primarily for people who are striving to take their book of business to the next level. This is the foundation for getting to—and staying at—the top.

Here's how it works:

- **Best Bets™ Opportunities**—These are the approximately 20 or so of your current clients and prospective new opportunities whom you can expect will make a decision in your current sales cycle. For some salespeople, the sales cycle is 30 to 90 days. For others, it's 12 to 18 months. And if you are in a national account or major opportunity environment, the sales cycle can be three to five years. In selling terms, this is also your "cross sell" opportunity with current clients, new relationships that look like your best clients or completely new opportunities. (Sometimes the Best Bets™ clients and new relationship opportunities are separated into two categories, depending on the industry.)

- **Future Best Bets™ Opportunities** — This represents future opportunities—both clients and prospective new opportunities—that you've identified outside of your current sales cycle. They are promising enough to keep an eye on. These are the opportunities you consider a significant part of your future success in terms of revenue and/or profit potential. These are clients who quite possibly could have a big future with you and you with them. This group varies from industry to industry and from salesperson to salesperson. Normally, you would not have more than 120 opportunities on your Future Best Bets™ list.

Once you have identified this list of Best Bets™ and Future Best Bets™ Opportunities, we recommend ranking them. Beside each name, rank them A, B or C. "A" would define your ideal target model client with very promising buying possibilities; "B" would denote an above-average client or new relationship in terms of buying potential; "C" clients are average to below-average potential. **Remove all the "C" opportunities, and focus only on opportunities ranked "A" and "B."** (Some of our rainmakers discard the "B" *and* "C" opportunities to focus their time and attention solely on the "A" opportunities.)

If you don't like the length or the quality of your list, don't worry. By focusing on fewer relationships, you will be able to channel your time, talents and resources to prospect, network and search out additional potential "A" clients and new relationships. **Remember, you are looking for a simple and effective model of success, not a confusing, overly demanding jumble of possibilities.**

Once you have identified your Best Bets™ (and Future Best Bets™) Opportunities, develop and implement your "drip marketing program" to systematically "touch" and work the targeted list. Remember, drip marketing possibilities include calls, emails, letters, brochures, newsletters, articles of interest, open houses, seminars, dinners, personal notes, appreciation gifts, etc. Delegate or outsource your touch program, when possible, and focus your time and talents on meeting with, talking to and communicating with your targeted few **Best Bets™**. Note: You focus your time and efforts on being an advisor to your clients and new relationships, and your staff, where applicable, supports and implements your high-touch programs.

During the course of a year, your Best Bets™ Opportunities continually change—growing and shrinking as referrals come in, people move away, companies get acquired, the economy changes and the market makes adjustments. **That is why developing your centers of influence and asking for referrals on a regular basis is so critical—it's a cornerstone for this model. You want to reduce your cold calling to a minimum.** Your goal is to make "warm" calls by finding a common connection with a new relationship. Our rainmakers continue to prove that establishing alliances with centers of influence (CPAs, attorneys, colleagues and consultants) and being an advisor to their clients provide them with an ongoing influx of new opportunities.

Another source of opportunities comes from just being active in the marketplace. **We encourage a mindset of abundance, which recognizes that opportunities could come from anywhere** including, but not limited to, your chamber of commerce, or civic, religious or social networks of people you know or who know you. These are not your Best Bets™ Opportunities that you will primarily focus on; you'll work them, but only as they come to you. **Our Best Bets™ Model proves that there is little money in the masses.** It's all about focusing on the right opportunities—and keeping an open mind concerning others.

Some of our rainmakers have developed some type of a drip marketing program with these types of contacts using mass mailings, newsletters, etc. If you decide to do this, have your office staff or a new salesperson work this group. It is a wonderful way to get a new salesperson started by having them focus on non-targeted opportunities. You spend your time elsewhere.

The rainmakers we know who follow this Best Bets™ Model of focusing on a few, select opportunities have plenty of business and it's business that is more likely to pay off.

What's more, because your Best Bets™ and Future Best Bets™ Opportunities will be a manageable number of clients on which to focus, you will reap the rewards in increased income and revenue as well as decreased stress. **Trust us, it works. And it's proven.** Best of all, if you consistently work the model, it gives you greater joy, freedom, income and time to create balance in your life.

Working with a select group of clients and new relationships using an advisory approach to the sales process requires that you look at your current book of business (and how you relate to those listed there) a little differently. **As you sharpen your focus on your future, you'll need to develop different habits.** Get rid of low revenue, slow paying, overly demanding relationships that hold you back or drain you of your energy. In short: **Work more strategically.** You might start by doing some of the following:

1. **Realize that all clients are not created equal.** Do not service work, call, visit or market to all your clients in the same way. Your "touch" program could be broken down into three categories. For example, you'll have high-, moderate- and low-touch programs—each of which is based on the size or potential importance of a client or new-relationship opportunity. Delegate all of them, if possible.

2. **Fire, ignore and give away 10 percent to 45 percent of your existing clients each year.** These are the ones that are problems when it comes to paying or being satisfied. They offer little in the way of significant future business. **Most salespeople can't do this because they don't have enough new-opportunity inventory.** Use the Best Bets™ Model and follow the abundance principle to provide you the freedom and flexibility to do what you want to do and back away from the shackles of working with draining, dead-end relationships.

3. **Focus on quality, not quantity, when it comes to clients.** Forget the "funnel" concept you learned in the past when you put as many opportunities into your "sales system" as possible. More is not better. It is only more, and it causes confusion about where and how you should spend your time, talents and efforts. Instead, focus on your Best Bets™ and Future Best Bets™ Opportunities. Just having **fewer opportunities will allow you to sharpen your focus and simplify your business life.** Nobody can focus fully on 1,000 prospects at once, but you *can* successfully work a selective number of opportunities.

4. **Be your clients' advisor.** Forget about trying to sell something to your clients. Think in terms of being an advisor to them. Average salespeople focus on their products and not on the clients' problems, challenges and opportunities. On the other hand, **rainmakers focus on how their products and services solve problems for the clients and help achieve their clients' goals.**

5. **Be the expert.** Specialize. Don't try to be all things to all people; instead, **strive to become *the* expert in your field.** Form strategic alliances with other firms to help your clients. Not only will you be more valuable to the clients, but you also will keep "friends" in your accounts and "foes" out by selecting who helps you.

We assist the salespeople in our coaching program in managing their Best Bets™ and Future Best Bets™ Opportunities. We provide a template for moving these opportunities through the sales process. If opportunities have not been identified with a group of relationships, the salesperson is responsible for obtaining and tracking industry databases, former client lists, country club memberships, chamber listings, etc. Our system helps you focus and close your current Best Bets™ and move your Future Best Bets™ Opportunities further along in the sales process.

As you build your relationships and demonstrate your ability to be an advisor to a Future Best Bets™ Opportunity, you'll know when to transition that client into a current, active, revenue-producing Best Bets™ Opportunity.

Year-Round High Activity

Rainmakers **actively look for ways to be advisors to their clients.** And they wisely develop and **follow a strategic sales plan** for working with select clients and new opportunities. **Rainmakers also thrive on activity.** They love being with clients; they look forward to forming new relationships. It's in their blood. Little wonder then that **the third component of our Best Bets™ Model is a working routine of high activity each and every day, all year round.**

As we talked about in the Fundamentals of Work for Salespeople chapter, high activity includes all the things that you do with clients and new relationships to first get on their radar and then demonstrate you can be a trusted advisor for them.

We believe that most of your working hours should be spent in front of and talking to your clients and new relationships. Remember, **to understand their business, you have to spend time at their business. To appreciate their challenges and opportunities, you have to talk with them—and listen.** In our sales coaching program, we track the number of face-to-face visits with program participants' Best Bets™ Opportunities. As we said earlier in the book, we do this not as "police work," but because it is one of the best indicators of success.

Most salespeople find it relatively easy to focus on and give attention to their existing clients—the weak spot for a lot of salespeople lies in developing new relationships. Our model emphasizes the importance of regularly adding additional clients through new opportunities. Remember, it's not *if* you lose that big client one day, but *when* you lose that client. You develop new relationships by spending time with them and working hard to understand their business. This calls for a high level of activity. Consistently.

We emphasize high activity not just "for the numbers." **High activity is how you keep your clients happy.** It's how you develop meaningful relationships. It's how you become an advisor. Work hard, keep your activity high (with current and new clients), and the success will follow.

Ongoing Accountability

By now you recognize **the importance of taking on an advisory role** with your clients. You know to **work with select clients and new opportunities via a strategic sales plan.** And you **realize how crucial high activity is to your success**. Those, of course, are the first three of the four components of our **Best Bets™ Model**.

The final factor of our model involves ongoing accountability.

Accountability is what keeps you in the game. Many salespeople work diligently to be an advisor to their clients. They develop a winning, strategic sales plan, and they focus their strategic efforts on select clients and new opportunities. Usually, they work very hard at this. But they are accountable, on a day-to-day basis, to no one but themselves. That's not enough.

What happens when you need to do more to understand your clients' changing needs? What happens when you need to review your strategic plan and make adjustments? Wouldn't it help to have someone there to watch your back? To keep you on track? To hold you responsible to your plan of action? Bottom line: **Accountability keeps you focused—on your clients, on your plan, on your activity and on your goals.** Rainmakers know that accountability is crucial to their success. In our coaching model, accountability keeps the rainmaker focused and working smart. Time and again, accountability reminds the rainmaker of what's really important.

It is imperative that you develop some type of accountability program for yourself. Perhaps you seek out a mentor; this person could be your manager or the company owner. You might look to an experienced and knowledgeable colleague at your company or an outside-of-the-company sales coach. Just make sure you find someone who is willing to be authentic with you and provide you with open, honest feedback. And make sure this is someone who can give you *accurate* feedback.

Don't pick a friend. Sometimes, feedback from friends is viewed as criticism. Often times, they tell you what you want to hear.

And yet, at the same time, we know that you "sharpen iron with iron." So seek out someone you respect, honor and trust but who isn't a buddy.

Here's something else we know absolutely: Leave out accountability, and you'll fall short of your goals and your dreams. Accountability—on a regular basis—is key to Doing What You Do Better.

Sales Stages of the Best Bets™ Opportunities Pipeline

We'd be remiss if we talked about the sales process and the Best Bets™ Pipeline and we didn't discuss sales stages. **In our advisory approach to sales, you have to understand where you are in the sales process at all times. Then you have to know where you're going next.**

Every company we work with has some variations and exceptions to the sales process. We've worked with organizations that had four simple steps to their sales method; others have more.

Here is a simplified Best Bets™ Sales Process:

1. Potential Opportunity (identified but have not met yet)
2. Prospect (have met; Future Best Bets™)
3. Assessing Their Business / Actively Gathering Information (Best Bets™)
4. Proposing / Recommending (Best Bets™)
5. Closing (Best Bets™)
6. Win / Loss / No Decision

From that simplified model, you can add multiple variations to the sales stages. The more advisory/consultative your role, the more stages you can establish. We've worked with people who have had 20 stages in their sales process.

Here is a more detailed Best Bets™ Sales Process:

1. New Opportunity
2. Pre-Approach
3. Initial Communication
4. First Interview
5. Opportunity Analysis
6. Solution Development
7. Solution Presentation
8. Client Evaluation
9. Negotiation
10. Commitment to Invest
11. Follow-up

Our only word of caution is to keep your sales process as simple and straightforward as possible. Traditionally, salespeople perform better if the sales stages are easy for them to understand and remember.

The purpose of any number of sales stages is to give everyone involved with a current or future opportunity a clear understanding of where you are in the sales process. The sales stages become the road map to moving the business forward. By documenting them, everyone is moving in the same direction.

Selling Success

"Successful selling is not just about getting the client to buy. Exceed their expectations, and become a partner in their success. You'll both come out winners."

— Marc Corsini

INSIDE

Sales Success: Corsini's 125 Sales Tips

As we've already discussed, success in sales, like in any other profession, depends upon how well you can execute the **Fundamentals** of your work. We're talking about those day-to-day tasks that add up to a job well done. Now, just about anyone can be successful at doing something for one hour or for one day. *True* success comes from focusing on and then successfully executing these fundamentals of work time after time, day after day.

The rainmakers we've coached have these **Fundamentals of Selling** well in hand. They know what works for them and how to work it. They've developed a sales *system*.

Through years of coaching these top producers, we've gleaned a number of tips that focus on the fundamentals of selling. You'll find 125 of them on the following pages. These tips come from thousands of coaching sessions with hundreds of rainmakers. They will show you that often your success comes down to *how* you work, not necessarily how *hard* you work. These ideas will help you go for quality not quantity in your face-to-face visits. You'll see the importance of focusing on the client's needs. And you'll realize the value of always being authentic. Do that and the client will trust you, and then the sale will come naturally.

There's something here for salespeople with all levels of experience.

For young and inexperienced salespeople, we challenge you to read, reread and then commit to memory the principles in this chapter. Quite simply: If you put them to work, they will certainly work for you.

Our rainmakers will find timely and useful reminders of highly effective techniques. You'll recognize ideas that might already have proven to be useful and profitable. You'll be reminded of others that perhaps you need to try again. And you'll surely find something new here, too.

You might want to take the time to read through all 125 sales tips in one sitting. There is a lot of information here, and a quick read-through will give you a foundation of understanding. Next, we suggest focusing on 10 tips at a time. You might take 10 tips each week and then incorporate them into your schedule and sales activities. Or you might want to take a larger, shared approach. Have your sales team read 10 tips and then discuss them in depth at a weekly sales meeting.

No matter what method you use, we suggest a systematic approach to putting these tips to work. Follow them with thought and focus. They will help you Do What You Do Better.

Sales Success:
Corsini's 125 Sales Tips

Rainmakers are always asking for tips and techniques they can use to do what they do better. In answer, many times over, the CCG coaches have compiled 125 of our favorite and most effective sales tips.

Working Smart

1. See the people.

Make at least one business-related appointment every business day. This allows you to move the business forward with at least one opportunity or referral source each day. Also, your sales-related skills will remain sharp.

2. Make success a habit.

Establish and maintain good working habits. Remember that it takes 21 days to establish a new, good habit and only five to seven days to lose an existing one.

3. Ask and you shall receive.

Asking for—and acting on—referrals is the most effective tool you have for moving your business forward. Get in the habit of asking for referrals. Then follow up on your leads. Also, ask every businessperson you talk with this: *"From a selling and business-development perspective, what's working for you?"*

4. Do what you do better.

Always keep productive reading or listening materials with you. That way you won't waste time in traffic, at the airport or in your office.

5. Take one step.

You don't have to move mountains. Instead, you just climb them one step at a time. Don't worry about the impossible; act on the possible.

6. Look inside.

"Inside a cold call is an appointment; inside the appointment is an objection; inside the objection is a need; and, finally, inside the need is a beautiful sale." (from a cartoon in the *Overcoming Objections* newsletter)

7. Move on.

Forget failures. When considering your performance, do you think about your successes or your failures? Continued rewinding and replaying of past loses causes despair, fear and call reluctance. Visualizing successes leads to confidence, assertiveness and positive self-esteem.

8. Be a Bubba.

In the movie *Forrest Gump*, Forrest's friend Bubba had a passion for shrimp. He lived, breathed and dreamed about shrimp. Be a Bubba. Be passionate about something. Be *the* expert, and success follows.

9. Expand your mind.

Read, watch and pay attention to "odd stuff." Talk to people in other fields. Ideas, opportunities, new products and new clients are everywhere and anywhere. Visit your local library, get on the Internet and read "stuff" that you normally would not read.

10. Dale's idea.

When faced with a difficult task (client problems, cold calls, getting a check from a client behind on paying, etc.) ask the question Dale Carnegie made famous, *"What is the worst thing that could happen from this situation?"* Answering this question places the problem in perspective and allows you to move to action.

11. **95 percent win rates.**

Whenever we hear a salesperson say, *"I win 95 percent of the times I engage in competition,"* our response is, *"I am sorry to hear that."* Winning most *all* the time indicates you are not competing enough. Likely, you only go after "safe" opportunities. You will never hit "the big, long-shot deal" with this attitude.

12. **Increase your at-bats.**

Just as in baseball, the more times at the plate (we're talking about face-to-face sales calls, phone calls, emails and proposals presented), the more hits (revenue, gross profit, money, new relationships) you will get.

13. **Too much white in your calendar?**

When sales are down, check your appointment book or electronic calendar to see how much open time you have during the day. Maybe you are not seeing enough people.

14. **Be authentic.**

Be authentic with all of your relationships. Period.

15. **Drive-by viewing.**

Want to know how many people work for your competition? Drive by, and count the number of cars in their parking lot. Do this two or three times. Notice the make of the cars. Often that's a reflection of the firm's prosperity.

16. **Be accountable.**

Be 100 percent accountable for your actions. Don't blame the boss, the economy, technology, the company or your products/services for any problem you encounter. Take responsibility for your own success.

17. **Put yourself in your clients' shoes.**

Have empathy. Care about what *they* want to accomplish. Understand their concerns, dreams, wishes and fears.

18. **Lead clubs.**

Organize or join a club of people in related but noncompetitive fields with the goal of sharing new opportunities and prospecting tips. (Make sure you join a club of "rainmakers." Clubs are not created equal—some are better than others.)

19. **Do the things you fear.**

   People often fear cold calling and rejection. Consequently, they don't prospect new opportunities enough, and they fall short of their revenue goals. Usually, doing something is better than doing nothing at all—even if your actions are not perfect. If you don't know how to do something, get training today.

20. **Practice Pareto's Law.**

   In 1895 Italian economist Vilfredo Pareto said, *"Eighty percent of the value comes from 20 percent of the efforts."* This idea still holds true and applies to many things—you probably wear 20 percent of your favorite clothing 80 percent of the time, and, likely, 80 percent of your selling success comes from 20 percent of your clients.

21. **Take charge.**

   Remember that *you* manage the sales call. You are the facilitator. Treat each call as an interview—and you are the interviewer.

22. **Create conflict.**

   Conflict is the difference between expectations and reality (performance). Expect people (and yourself) to perform at a higher level, and they (and you) will.

23. **Automate your sales process.**

   Use one of the many electronic contact relationship management (CRM) systems to increase your productivity, aid in your Best Bets™ Opportunities, and automatically provide you and management with your sales-process reporting.

24. **Continuous improvements.**

   Henry Ford said, *"The only thing worse than losing a trained employee is keeping an untrained one."* Attend some type of professional development every six months to fulfill your life-long commitment to doing what you do better.

25. **Keep 'em happy.**

   Unhappy clients are expensive negative advertising. Studies show unhappy clients complain to eight people, while satisfied customers boast to three.

26. Look alike.

Generally, your best opportunities look like your best clients. Learn to recognize that look, and then focus on the look-alike.

27. Love your work.

Do what you love to do, and commit to becoming excellent at it. The financial and/or emotional rewards will follow. Discover the right livelihood for yourself, and the rest will take care of itself.

28. Clean up your act.

Keep your office, car and work area clean. If they are dirty or messy, that gives the appearance of lack of detail and laziness.

29. Create your own franchise plan.

Create and execute a strategic sales plan for yourself. If you were a franchise and we looked at your sales business plan, would we buy your franchise or would we take a pass?

30. Big differences.

Focus on your uniqueness. Figure out what you and your company do best, and focus on doing that. Don't try to do everything. Become *the* best at something.

31. Dine out.

Eat out with clients and new relationships as often as possible. There is a classic adage: *"Do you know the most expensive lunch a salesperson can have? It's one with three other salespeople."* It's hard to sell to someone who sells the same thing you do. Remember, you need to eat breakfast and lunch, and you might as well spend some portion of those meals developing or nurturing relationships and demonstrating to them that you are an advisor to their success.

32. In focus.

Focus on outcomes and results. Learn the client's desired outcome, and make that outcome your solution.

33. Write it right.

Take notes during a sales call, and keep records for future use.

34. Hindsight is 20/20.

Evaluate each call. Ask yourself what worked and what went wrong. Determine or find out how to correct your mistakes and emphasize your strengths. And take time to routinely evaluate your advisory approach to sales.

35. Encountering *"no."*

Remember, if you are trying to add new clients you likely will hear *"no"* 95 percent of the time. Stop worrying and don't get discouraged when you hear the word *"no."* Concentrate on turning it into *"yes"* or moving on to the next opportunity.

36. Keeping score.

Make sure you are working with enough Best Bets™ Opportunities (clients and new relationships) to achieve (and better yet, overachieve) your goals. Determine whether your opportunity pipeline is growing sufficiently (know whom to add and whom to delete). Also, define the number of face-to-face meetings, proposals, demos, and wins/loses that must be made in order to achieve your goals.

37. Hurrah for you!

Be your own cheerleader and coach to keep active and energetic when involved in a task.

38. Never quit.

Be persistent but not obnoxious. Know the difference between the two.

Communicating

39. Hour of power!

Use the telephone wisely every day. Set aside time daily to develop and increase your relationships using the phone. Make one more call every day than you feel comfortable making. Soon you'll raise your "telephone-pain threshold."

40. Head gear.

Wear a headset to call people. You will be more comfortable and productive, better able to make notes, and you won't have the tendency to procrastinate. Also, stand up. We sound more confident while standing up.

41. Voice-mail messages.

Start with a "headline" when leaving a voice-mail message. By quickly and briefly explaining the nature of your call, the recipient can decide whether to listen to the remainder of the message and if they want to take action.

42. Party lines.

Get everyone involved when demonstrating your "value add" to a new relationship. Have your IT manager, customer-service representative, president, administrative manager, etc. give the prospective client a call. Let them explain how *they* can help the client, too.

43. Think on your feet.

Don't panic when someone asks you a difficult question or makes a request and you're not prepared to answer. Give yourself time to respond by saying, *"That is a great question."* Or, *"Let me think about it, and I'll answer in a minute."* Or say, *"I'll write down your question now and ask someone back at the office how we can best help you."* Don't try to wing it.

44. Be an information sponge.

Constantly solicit information from your clients, new relationships, suppliers, trade groups, etc. Include short questionnaires with invoices, place suggestion cards and "How'd we do?" notes with correspondence so clients can easily and quickly let you know what kind of job you're doing. Hire a market-research firm, and have the folks there contact your clients.

45. Beware of the 500-pound receiver.

Don't hang up the receiver between telephone calls. You'll avoid interruptions by quickly pressing the button down and dialing your next call. Also, informal studies show that if you put the receiver down, procrastination often sets in and causes you to look for something else to do rather than make that next call.

46. "Y'all come see us."

Send postcards to people *before* you go to a trade show. Include dates, times and your booth location. This increases traffic at the show, and it keeps your name in front of those people who don't attend.

47. **Simply smile.**

Smile when leaving messages. You'll have an upbeat-sounding message that stands out from other "call me back" messages.

48. **Getting attention.**

Capture your readers' attention with the first sentence of your letters. Studies show the opening sentence of your direct-mail letter is the most important part of the entire letter.

49. **Don't ask.**

Avoid trite sayings such as *"How are you doing today?"* when calling people. It sounds phony and alerts people that you're a salesperson. Identify yourself in a professional manner, give your name and company name, and lead with something of interest.

50. ***"To be honest with you."***

Avoid the phrases *"honestly"* and *"to tell you the truth"* when talking with people. Think about what that says to people. Has everything up to that point been dishonest? (We know that's not what you meant, but still.) Use *"candidly"* and *"as a matter of fact"* to emphasize your points.

51. **Conference calls and video conferencing.**

Use conference calls and video teleconferencing as an inexpensive and readily accessible means of bringing people together. You'll avoid travel-related expenses, save time, and provide resources needed to educate or solve problems for current opportunities you are working on.

52. **Talk about "us."**

When giving a presentation, replace the words "I" and "me" with "we" and "us." People will feel you're working toward a common goal. *"I need you to order the product..."* doesn't sound like teamwork; *"We can start the process as soon as we have your signed agreement,"* does.

53. **Keep in touch.**

When going out of town on business, send an email to your best clients informing them of this. In the text, ask if there is something they would like for you to do for them while you are in that area. They'll be impressed that you are thinking of them.

54. Congratulations.

Anytime you read, hear or see something positive about someone, send them a note or email them about it. Congratulate them on their successes. They will be much more receptive to you when you approach them next time.

55. Share the wealth.

Always provide value when you meet, see and talk to people. Give them an idea, an improvement, a new approach to problems. Always add value. Do not waste people's time.

56. No dead letters.

Include the words "*Address Service Requested*" on all mailings if you plan to continue additional mailings. With this service, the post office will forward the mail, if possible, and then send you notification of the new address. There is a charge for each address update, but it's worth it.

57. Extra, extra—send newsletters.

People *do* read them. Consider mailing, posting to your Website or emailing informative newsletters regularly. Today, there are several services you can use to send out correspondence "automagically." Just tell them who you want to send to, what you want to send, when you want to do it and how often. They'll take care of the rest.

58. Picking up signals.

Know, read and respond to body language. It's a sure way to gauge a person's interest.

59. I object.

Be prepared to counter any objections. The more game experience you have, the better you will be at handling objections.

60. Perfect endings.

End each sales call with a "call to action" such as a signature on a contract, another appointment or an agreement to talk on the telephone, etc. And recognize that sometimes the "call to action" will be no future action required.

61. Listen up.

Never interrupt someone. God gave you two ears and one mouth. You should listen twice as much as you talk.

62. Follow up with a call.

Calling people after you have sent them direct-mail pieces can double your response rate.

63. Call on the president.

It was good advice 30 years ago, and it is still sound today. You can always go down the organizational chart, but once you start somewhere in the middle it's hard to go up.

64. Avoid sharks.

Call people in the early mornings and after hours. Normally, the "telephone screening sharks" won't be there, and you'll get through. As a rule of thumb, executives and entrepreneurs either come in early or work late.

65. Play the odds.

Typically, 10 calls will yield one face-to-face appointment.

66. *"There you are!"*

When visiting with people, do you have a *"There you are!"* or a *"Here I am!"* attitude when you first see them? People like to feel special. A *"There you are!"* kind of greeting will do it.

67. Wish you were here.

While on vacation, send your best clients thank-you notes telling them you appreciate their business and you value your relationship.

68. *"I hear you, BUT..."*

When someone is complaining about your company, product or service, resist the temptation to justify or defend yourself. Listen actively, take notes, and think in terms of a solution or improvement. This is contrary to what you will want to do. Salespeople think in terms of overcoming objections. Remember that an angry client might leave permanently.

69. *"Hello again, I'm Marc Corsini with Corsini Consulting Group."*

When seeing people in business settings you know only casually, always state your name and the company or service you represent. They will appreciate the subtle reminder; and after a while they will remember your name. Except for close relationships, we recommend doing that with all of your encounters in business and social settings.

70. **Throwback to the past—fax fixes.**

Tired of leaving a message with the secretary or on voice-mail? Try faxing your message with your reason for calling. Don't forget to emphasize the benefits to the client—not your product or service. Surprisingly, faxing might sometimes be more effective than emailing with today's overloaded in-boxes.

71. **Don't email or fax proposals.**

As a general rule, don't email or fax high-dollar proposals—especially to potential new clients. If it was worth your time to prepare a proposal, it's worth *their* time to see you face-to-face.

72. ***"Pardon me?"***

If people regularly ask you to identify yourself again after you state your name and company, you might be talking too fast. Slow down. Then give them your name and company name again toward the end of the call.

73. **Get involved.**

Get the new relationships involved in the sales process. Relationships and sales take time. Use a combination of phone calls, letters, faxes and email messages between face-to-face meetings.

74. **Be diplomatic to everyone.**

When making sales calls, be as gracious to the receptionist as you are to the president. We've heard time and again about assistants who eventually become the bosses. Who can blame them for firing the salesperson who was rude or ignored them before the promotion?

75. **Getting formal.**

Err on the side of formality when using people's names. College buddies might call the person "Hambone," but that doesn't automatically give you the right to do the same.

76. **Getting personal.**

Be personable in your correspondence with people. Avoid "corporate speak" such as, *"We at Corsini Consulting Group, LLC..."* Build a relationship between the prospect and you—not between the prospect and your company.

77. Warm up the room.

Ease into follow-up calls. Remind the person(s) of previous conversations, notes and commitments.

78. Table talk.

Invite current and new relationships to your office for a meal. It will give you a chance to show them your office, your team, etc. and develop the relationship(s) at the same time.

79. Network constantly.

Join trade, civic, social and professional organizations. Talk with the rainmakers and movers and shakers in your field. Ask them for advice—and stay in touch. Continuously expand your center of influence.

80. Be specific about what you want.

According to Bob Burg, author of *Endless Referrals: Network Your Everyday Contacts into Sales,* you should be specific when asking for a referral. Do not use the vague line, *"Do you know of anyone I should talk to?"* Help the person help you by narrowing his or her frame of reference. Consider asking specific questions such as, *"Do you know of a small- to medium-sized entrepreneurial company in this area that is growing beyond its internal expertise?"*

81. Win or lose, send an old-fashioned thank-you note.

Send a handwritten thank-you note every time you compete on a proposal—win or lose. Sending a thank-you note when you *lose* shows you have class and you appreciate the opportunity and the person. Plus you'll stand out.

82. Make the most of a move.

When moving or changing phone numbers, imprint your company's new information in a letter, brochure, email, etc. and distribute these items to people within your circle of influence. Also, consider sending postcards, novelty items and e-cards announcing your move. Use your move as an opportunity to communicate with current and potential relationships.

83. Avoid chitchat.

Ignore the office chitchatters and hall talkers. Be in the habit of making conversation with external relationships, not the office gossip.

84. Modest expectations.

Under-promise and over-deliver. It's a great way to keep 'em satisfied.

85. Plan it out.

Have a pre-call game plan every time you make any type of call. Know what you want to accomplish. Then, have a post-game plan, too.

Marketing

86. Just pennies a day.

Justify the cost (return on investment) of whatever you are offering. Explain how your products/services will help their business. Show the cost savings, productivity benefits and revenue increases.

87. More than just a name.

Use your business cards, letterhead, email signature, etc. as tools to communicate what your company offers—especially if your company has a name that doesn't give a clue as to what you do. Don't make people try to figure it out. Tell them!

88. Recent purchases.

According to database experts, people who have bought from you *recently* are statistically much more likely to respond to a new offer than someone who had made a purchase a long time ago. Spend more time, money and energy on these recent clients.

89. Follow up after the call.

After talking to someone, send some type of correspondence such as email, fax or an "old-fashioned" letter with a formal introduction and a brief description of what you offer. The repetition will help your sales efforts, increase your brand's awareness and keep you "top of mind" with the potential relationship.

90. Team work.

Team your outside salespeople with inside salespeople. Have a fluid strategy between them. Maybe the inside salespeople can send out routine information, introduction letters and product literature while the outside salespeople are making sales calls, executing contracts and uncovering new opportunities.

91. Contact 250 new relationships a year.

Try following up with five new people a week. A typical year has about 50 working weeks, so if you are disciplined and systematic, you'll get there.

92. Tag along.

Ask your clients if you may include your company brochure when they send out their statements. You'll create additional opportunities with little investment. In return for helping you out, provide the clients with incentives such as discounts and training seminars.

93. Clients on board.

Create and maintain a "client board of directors." Make it informal, informative and meet regularly with a planned agenda. Use the sessions as a chance to gain insights into their needs, frustrations and attitudes. Another version of this is a "board of advisors." Similar to a board of directors but more informal and less structured, in the right format and situation, it can be extremely beneficial.

94. Put a face with the name.

Include your photograph on brochures, flyers, press releases and articles submitted. Folks like to do business with people they can relate to and see as "managers." We live in a visual society. Also, most contact-managers today allow you to add pictures of your contacts. Keep a camera with you on calls, and take photos of your valued relationships.

95. Speaking of clients.

Take advantage of your clients' testimonials. Get them to write their positive comments down, or take notes and write their comments down for them. Also, consider videotaping their comments.

96. Elevator messages.

Create a 15-second commercial that succinctly states what you do for a living. The statement should define your business, your type of clients and the results people can expect from you. It's called an "elevator message" because you should be able to recount what you do in the time it takes to ride an elevator to another floor.

97. Simply centralize.

Centralize your Best Bets™ Opportunities and contact information (database). Relationships will be much easier to manage and produce if you keep your contact info in *one* place. Continuously update the information. Do it every day if necessary.

98. Outsource your mail.

Use a mail-fulfillment house for large mailings. They are inexpensive, experienced in dealing with the post office and they have bulk-mail permits.

99. Hello, stranger.

When out of the office networking for new opportunities or expanding your circle of influence, spend 80 percent of your time with people you *do not know* and 20 percent on current relationships.

100. All for a good cause.

Donate your product or service as a door prize for trade shows, civic auctions and your target-market industry organization. If what you offer isn't appropriate for the event, consider DVD players, iPods, etc. that were paid for by your company. The cooler the prize, the more memorable for the company.

101. Here's my card.

Include your business card when paying bills, sending invoices and in general correspondence, when appropriate.

102. Be *the* expert.

Become a "guru" in your industry. Seek out speaking engagements, write articles, teach a class, write a book and become an active member of your trade industry group. Be the "go-to" person in your industry.

103. Pay attention to your mail.

Before you just throw out your junk mail, ask yourself, *"How has direct mail changed over the past year? What trends are developing?"* And most importantly, *"How can I utilize these new trends in my correspondence?"*

104. Happy anniversary to you!

Take advantage of your company's anniversaries. Especially the 10th, 15th, 20th, etc. It doesn't cost much, and it is proof of your longevity. Stick-on seals denoting your anniversary can be attached to stationery, brochures, invoices, etc.

105. Promote locally.

Advertise in regional and local business magazines, newsletters, church bulletins, civic and volunteer newsletters, etc. It is a good reminder for people who already know you and who might need what you offer.

106. New channels.

Develop alternative ways (channels) to sell your products or services. If you have outside salespeople calling on businesses, consider starting a division selling over the Internet.

107. Produce a movie.

Are people too busy to read your literature or newsletters? Consider putting your message on your company's Website, on a CD, DVD or on YouTube. That way, people can get your message while in their cars, at home, at the office or while on vacation.

108. Say, "cheese."

Take pictures of clients using your products for your reference materials. Use their quotes, photos and stories to verify and support your claims.

Selling

109. Create success.

Create special deals, pricing arrangements and packages during your downtime or slow times. Boat dealers have been doing this for years by hosting boat shows during the winter—which is the slowest time of the year for boating.

110. Tupperware parties.

Preview new products, models and value-added services for existing clients at preferred-client shows. Keep it light, friendly, informative and fun.

111. "Free, free, free."

Use magic words like "free," "no-risk," "guaranteed" and "limited-time offer" to tempt people to buy. Avoid the small print with all types of disclaimers whenever possible. The stronger the offer, the more likely people will buy. Offering a money-back guarantee is as strong as it gets.

112. Sell memories.

Remember the classic sales adage to sell the "sizzle" and not the "steak." Kodak used to say that they made film—but they "sold memories."

113. Quote prices.

Do not give exact pricing over the telephone. But remember, failure to give any pricing or being evasive breaks down trust with people. You can give a range of prices and use pricing as a way to determine if there is an opportunity.

114. Sell futures.

Don't forget to sell future events, products, classes, etc. to people. During a World Skating Tour held throughout the United States, people at the event were asked to order tickets for the next year's tour. There were no announced dates nor were there any guarantees, just the opportunity to get what the organizers called "preferred priority tickets."

115. Product knowledge.

Know your product. Then know the competition's product. *Never* talk negatively about your competition, but be able to clearly differentiate between what you offer and what they offer.

116. Conduct dress rehearsals.

Before someone arrives for any type of presentation, demo or client visit, do a quick run-through in advance. Have an agenda with contacts, titles and a timeline. Distribute a copy to everyone involved. Give them instructions or suggestions about what you want each of them to cover.

117. Success times two.

Use two types of media to keep a meeting focused. You might use a flip chart to document the to-dos and the main outline of your meeting. And then you could use a PowerPoint presentation for background information or future objectives. This system makes it easier to focus on the desired outcome. And it keeps people's attention.

118. Perfect practice makes perfect.

Several surveys confirm that effective executives ranked communication and presentation skills as the No. 1 factor contributing to their success.

Time Management

119. Be selfish with your time.

Try to spend every available minute of your day on urgent and important tasks—especially those involving current and new opportunities. Delegate the rest. Simply don't do the ones that don't really matter.

120. Timing is everything.

Schedule an appointment on Friday afternoons and Monday mornings with someone you are pretty sure will lead to a positive outcome like moving the business forward. Your confidence will increase, and you will end and begin each week on a positive note.

121. Keep it short.

Try to limit your actual presentation to 20 minutes then allow time for questions, and you usually will stay within the optimal half-hour to forty-five minute timeframe. When multiple people are giving presentations, this is even more critical.

122. Time allotment.

Tell people in advance how much time you need for your conference call, presentation or demonstration. Then keep your promise. If you find yourself going over the time allotted, for whatever reason, ask them for more time or schedule a time to continue the presentation.

123. Add an extra month to your year.

Increase your productivity by one hour a day each working day, and you will add the equivalent of 28 eight-hour workdays in a year's time.

124. You gotta wanna.

After working with thousands of salespeople, we've learned the most important ingredient to success is the desire to be successful. You gotta wanna get there. Next, it takes discipline, resiliency and ongoing game experience.

125. Live a life of abundance.

Our experience is that people who are underachieving are living a life of scarcity, and rainmakers come at life from the standpoint of abundance. Rainmakers find opportunities at every turn because they are constantly looking for them. Also, they *expect* to find them. Underachievers overwork current opportunities, don't seek out new opportunities and depend on luck to be successful. Live a life of abundance (both in and out of the office), and you will forever be doing what you do better.

Winning Presentations

*"The most exciting presentation tools available
are only as good as the person using them."*
— Marc Corsini

INSIDE

Bits, Bytes and Timely Tips for Perfecting Your Presentations

With today's high-speed, highly portable technology, a winning presentation is literally right at your fingertips. But good, old-fashioned preparedness still has a place in modern presentations. Without it, you could be tripped up by something as simple as an extension cord.

As we all become more media savvy (and saturated), presentations have become more complex. And with that complexity come new problems to be solved.

One thing about a successful presentation that hasn't changed: **You've got to present something that captures your audience's attention and makes them want to listen to what you have to say.**

As a sales professional, you'll be called upon, sooner or later or even regularly, to put together and then present information to your clients. This is fundamental to your success in sales. As we all become more accustomed to the loads of new information we receive in the course of an ordinary day, it's just going to become more difficult to make what you have to say stand out. Audiences today, whether they are business clients or church members, want to be entertained and learn something at the same time. The entertainment value is almost as important as the content in some of today's presentations.

You'll need to keep this in mind as you prepare your presentation. Also, realize that a presentation has a beginning, a middle and an end. Each of these parts needs to be strong:

- **The introduction**: Be enthusiastic, and thank your audience for having you there. Be sure to give a quick acknowledgment to the people who made that happen.
- **The main point**: Be clear and concise with your information. Emphasize your expertise as an advisor, and talk up how what you offer can help the client do what they do better.
- **The conclusion**: Summarize your main points, highlight once more the benefits of doing business with your firm and thank your audience sincerely.
- **The Q&A session**: Try to anticipate important questions that are likely to be asked. Keep your answers brief and on point. If you don't know the answer, don't fake it. Tell the person you'll get back with them.

And you should know that there is a formula to point you in the direction of a winning presentation. It's called the "10/20/30 PowerPoint rule of thumb." According to Microsoft, PowerPoint produces more than 30 million presentations worldwide every day. The 10/20/30 PowerPoint rule of thumb says a PowerPoint presentation should have 10 slides, the presentation should last no more than 20 minutes and it should contain no font smaller than 30 points.

Now, whether you present your information with PowerPoint, through virtual presentations via Webcast or teleconference, or with charts and a projector, is up to you. Increasingly, people are turning to online solutions like Google Presentations with their cool animation and easy video integration.

As you prepare, consider how you can extend the conversation you start with your presentation. Maybe you can share portions of your presentation through interactive tools like your client's company intranet. Web-savvy audiences often want to interact. Give them the means to do so.

Just remember to use technology that makes you feel comfortable. Giving a presentation can be nerve-wracking enough as is without using a tool or technology you don't know well. And speaking of nerves, don't worry about having butterflies; just make sure yours are flying in formation.

Whatever tools you use, and however far you extend your message, the tips on the next few pages can help make your presentations easier and more effective.

Following the advice in these tips will result in better, stronger and more effective presentations. And this will help you Do What You Do Better.

Bits, Bytes and Timely Tips for Perfecting Your Presentations

The following tips—technical and common sense—will help you and your audience get the most from your next presentation:

1. **Advance notice.**

   Prepare an agenda in advance, and gain approval with everyone (especially the client) before continuing the presentation. And know exactly how much time you'll have available for your presentation.

2. **Have an outline.**

   You don't have to follow an outline religiously, but you can use it to prompt you when discussion or questions interrupt your flow.

3. **Practice makes perfect.**

   Rehearse every part of your presentation from set-up to the Q & A session. Practice in front of a mirror, and read your presentation out loud. Better yet, practice in front of a friend or colleague who can give you constructive feedback. Pay attention to your voice—your most valuable tool as a presenter. Don't be too loud, and mind the tone, pitch and pace of your talk.

4. **Have a look around.**

   Preview the room in which you'll give your presentation; do this 24 hours in advance, if possible. And make sure you arrive at least two hours before any important presentation. If possible, conduct a dry run of your presentation in the room where you'll be presenting.

5. **Know your audience.**

   Consider what they need from you, and use terminology they'll understand. Know their business jargon, but don't use it too much. Sprinkle it into your presentation for greatest impact.

6. **Stay focused.**

   You must narrow the focus of your presentation to what's important to your audience. Don't bombard them with information. Since you are the presenter, they know you are the expert; you don't have to prove it to them.

7. Personality plus.

Presentations allow the speaker's personality to shine and facilitate immediate interaction between the speaker and the audience. A good presentation will carry more weight than a good report because of the person giving it.

8. Don't talk to strangers.

Establish a rapport with the audience before the presentation begins by greeting people individually as they enter the room. You'll connect before you even begin.

9. Listen up.

Use the casual greeting time before the presentation to chat with people, keeping your ears open for information that might bolster your presentation. Use that information to personalize and customize your presentation by recalling a conversation between you and one of the audience members about something pertinent to the audience you're addressing.

10. What do they want?

Before you even begin, establish the client's goals and your goals for the presentation. Write them down, and refer to them often. Don't leave the meeting before reviewing and verifying whether the goals have or have not been met.

11. Where do you stand?

Know where your Best Bets™ Opportunity is in their decision-making process. If you are the first of several presenters, they likely will not make a firm decision directly after you finish. Don't worry about it. Better yet, try to be the final presenter. Your message will remain fresh when the client is ready to make a decision.

12. Back to basics.

It is absolutely essential that you don't get so caught up in sexy technology that you forget the basics. The best computer graphics in the world won't matter if you need an electrical socket and it's out of reach. Pay attention to the smallest details.

13. **Mix master.**

Enhance your presentations with clever uses of newspaper clippings, cartoons, music, appropriate quotes or relevant experiences. Use your imagination. At a minimum, do something as simple as writing descriptive captions for slides rather than just giving them titles.

14. **Be flexible.**

Clients' needs often change between your initial contact and the final presentation. Make sure you're ready and prepared to make any necessary changes.

15. **Equip yourself.**

Make sure you have a "technology jock" with you for important presentations or at least have someone available by telephone who knows your technology and communications needs.

16. **Double up.**

For a "jumbo" opportunity, take two extension cords and two copies of your presentation on removable media. And since Murphy was a speaker, take a hard copy that you can hand out. If everything goes wrong, at least you'll have that.

17. **Don't get too comfortable.**

Beware of a false sense of security. Unless you are dealing with an audio/visual professional, do not assume anything will be ready for you. Most people do not understand your needs for presenting a high-tech talk.

18. **Mind the details.**

Make sure your environment is in your favor. Adjust the thermostat so the presenters and audience are comfortable, check for flip-chart paper and usable pens, monitor outside noises, etc.

19. **Help yourself.**

Put everyone at ease by providing snacks, drinks, fruit, etc. If the presentation takes more than 30 to 45 minutes, plan for breaks. Don't provide heavy foods—they make people sleepy.

20. A picture is worth a thousand words.

Make your presentation as visually pleasing as possible. Use images whenever you can. Make your message more appealing with some type of audio/visuals such as interactive white boards, overhead transparencies, flip charts, slides, posters, large screens/monitors, etc.

21. Time does matter.

Get to your point quickly; stay within your time limit; and avoid complex, difficult-to-understand presentations. If you're given 45 minutes for your meeting, plan on a 30-minute presentation and leave 15 minutes for questions, answers and surprises.

22. No feature presentation.

Don't ramble on about every feature of your product or service. In fact, don't focus on the features. Instead, **point out how they will help your client succeed.**

23. Solicit input.

After major points, get some audience reaction. Ask how what you've just presented will help the client or how it can be improved. This back and forth makes for a relaxed presentation and keeps your audience focused.

24. It's not about you.

Put yourself in your client's shoes. Build your presentation around *their* needs and wants. Emphasize what your product or service does for *them and their company*. Bottom line: Concentrate on your client's problems and your solutions to those problems, and the sale will naturally follow.

25. Be authentic.

If you don't know the answer to a question, don't fake it. No one knows everything, and there's nothing wrong with telling the person you'll get back to them personally with the answer to their question. **Always be authentic with your clients.** Always!

26. Stay off the Internet.

A real-time visit to the Internet sounds exciting, but there are just too many things that can go wrong. Besides, it's just too complex; in addition to a modem, you also need a good telephone line or Wi-Fi, a reliable Internet connection, and the site has to be up and running. It's just too much to deal with. If showing a Website is crucial to your presentation, save the pages and graphics on your computer.

27. Don't let computers replace creativity.

Technology can become gimmicky, and sometimes it's downright distracting. Let your creative ability shine—not just your technical savvy.

28. Engage your audience.

Remember, we are influenced only 10 percent by what we hear and 90 percent by what we see and feel. Engage the audience. Include slides with questions directed to your audience during the presentation. This keeps your audience involved, and it checks their retention of the information. Maybe even give prizes for correct answers.

29. Oops.

If any or all of your equipment fails, have an emergency plan. Have back-up plans for broken audio/visual equipment, late presenters, early clients and anything else you think might happen. Bring handouts or charts—anything to get your point across. Don't make excuses for the problem; act as though nothing has gone wrong. Likewise, if you make a mistake, don't let the way you handle it compound the error. If you shrug it off and move on, the audience most likely will, too. Anticipate problems, and you'll be ready for them.

30. Don't just stand there, do something.

Once the presentation is under way, move around the room rather than staying planted behind a lectern. This makes you seem more accessible. Also, make eye contact. But don't just focus on the decision-maker. Assistants and secretaries might also have some say in what happens next.

31. Special delivery.

Your poise, gestures and speaking ability will reflect on your competence and your product's quality. For a really important presentation, videotape yourself delivering the presentation and evaluate the tape for ways to improve. You also might want to seek professional coaching in order to improve your presentation technique.

32. "That's a good question."

Don't let the "um's" and "ah's" ruin a great presentation. You can use statements like "That's a really good question" or "I'm so glad you asked that" to buy some time while you organize your thoughts during the Q&A session. Also, this affirms the person who asked the question.

33. Get feedback.

Hand out an evaluation form after the presentation so you can get feedback on how you did. But don't get defensive about the evaluation comments. Learn from them; don't try to justify your mistakes. This allows you to get better and better.

34. Murphy was right.

Things will go wrong, but be tenacious. When you branch out into more technically challenging presentations, chances are you'll experience some problems at first. But anticipating problems allows room for error, and the problems themselves allow room for growth. Don't get discouraged and fall back into the comfort zone of a podium and 3x5 cards.

35. Have fun.

To persuade other people, you must connect with them on a personal level. If you enjoy what you're doing, they will recognize this and are more likely to respond favorably. You must believe that what you have to say is important—because it is. If you present your information with enthusiasm and a firm belief in yourself and your company, you'll deliver a successful presentation and make a lasting, favorable impression at the same time.

Joint Ventures: Corsini's Guide to Negotiating

"In sales and in life, a successful and significant negotiation is truth-based, fair and ultimately mutually beneficial to all parties."

— Marc Corsini

INSIDE

Joint Ventures: Corsini's Guide to Negotiating for What You Want in Sales (and in Life)

Sample Negotiation

If you live and work with the abundance principle in mind, sooner or later, you'll find yourself in a negotiation situation. Opportunities, no matter how abundant, aren't always there for the quick picking. Sometimes you have to negotiate for them.

Matter of fact, life is full of disagreements and differences, concessions and compromises. You might run into contract disagreements and have to make price concessions. You might navigate a disagreement over compensation one day at work and later that same day deal with a bedtime compromise at home with your child. Being a skillful negotiator impacts many areas of your life—in and out of the office.

We believe negotiating to be of such importance to a rainmaker's arsenal of work tools that we're giving you an entire chapter on achieving effective negotiations in sales. We're giving you the means to help you avoid "an old-fashioned whipping" in an important negotiation with a potential client or a current one; we'll show you how to avoid being emotionally "held hostage" over specific terms and conditions of an agreement.

Being a good negotiator means you can meet your needs while working to ensure that the other person's needs are met as well. How do you do this? First of all, you approach the process by taking responsibility for the success or failure of the negotiation. **You enter into a negotiation situation with truth as your guiding principle; you should act in a spirit of fairness; and you should strive for an outcome that is mutually beneficial to all parties involved.** Many people go into a negotiation thinking that there will be winners and losers. That's not the goal. That will not serve you well in the long run, and it doesn't foster good working relationships. A win-win situation is what you're after.

It all comes back to this idea of abundance. Not just for you, but for the other party, too. If you approach any negotiation in this way, over time, you will be known as someone who is fair, authentic and trustworthy. If you don't, well, you will be seen as self-serving, false and dishonest. (And maybe some other descriptions that are even worse.)

A lot of salespeople today are ill-equipped to negotiate effectively and successfully. So, on the following pages, we'll look at the various aspects of a successful negotiation. We also offer proven, productive techniques and ideas for negotiating and resolving conflict quickly and effectively in almost any situation.

But know this: We are not offering silver bullets or tricks. There are no constant answers or concrete ways to handle complex negotiations—every situation is different. Participants vary. On the other hand, if you're looking for a proven *process* to help you (and others) get what you want in a sales situation and in life outside the office—you will be satisfied.

Go into every negotiation with the abundance principle in mind, and use our Joint Ventures model. I can assure you that you will Do What You Do Better.

Joint Ventures:
Corsini's Guide to Negotiating
for What You Want in Sales (and in Life)

What comes to mind when you think of a complex negotiation? Problems? Differences? Battles? Anger? Anxiety?

Did you happen to notice that these words all have a negative connotation? That's because **negotiating, especially in a significant sales situation, is often perceived as a *negative* occurrence.** And that doesn't need to be the case. Negotiating is a way to give *all* parties what they ultimately desire in any given situation.

Our mission is to provide you with a proven, *proactive* model to help you successfully negotiate present and future opportunities and situations. This model works with existing clients as well as new relationships. It also works with co-workers, managers and vendors—whomever you interact with in sales. As a matter of fact, our ideas even apply to negotiations you might have at church, at the ballpark or within your own family. But since we are focusing on the **Fundamentals of Work for Salespeople**, we'll primarily look at how these ideas help you succeed in the workplace.

Better Than Nothing?

Historically, salespeople have been given very few lessons on how to negotiate during the selling process. And if they have attended any type of negotiating training, it has probably involved negotiation seminars with names such as:

- "*Knowledge is Power*"
- "*Win the War: Tips to Win Your Battles in Business*"
- "*Negotiate Your Way to #1*"

These titles offer a great jumping-off point for discussing why manipulation and tricks aren't effective. First, let's look at "*Knowledge is Power.*" This idea is based on the concept of "he who has the most information has the advantage." Now, being informed is a positive thing. And in a negotiation, having truth-based information is absolutely necessary. **But information is just one part of a negotiation.** It is by no means the be-all-and-end-all.

The "*Win the War*" approach to negotiating implies that there must be winners and losers. According to this model, one party is dominant and the other is submissive. Perhaps this is what Frederick Sawyer had in mind when he lightheartedly defined a contract as "*an agreement that is binding only on the weaker party.*" **You can't establish successful, productive, *long-term* relationships in sales by having winners and losers.** That's why our model is not a winner-takes-all-approach.

Finally, the "*Negotiate Your Way to #1*" model defines negotiating as a game where each party jockeys to see which demands and interests will be traded, eliminated and obtained. Success is measured either by how little was given up or by how much was obtained. **Partnership doesn't exist in this method of negotiating.**

Interestingly, one of the most popular approaches to negotiating has nothing at all to do with any of the aforementioned methods. I'm talking about avoidance. **Given the choice, most people would *avoid negotiating whenever possible*.** The idea is that if you ignore the situation, sooner or later the other party will lose interest and simply go away or perhaps the situation will magically come to a successful resolution. I can tell you, from coaching people through hundreds of negotiations, situations rarely—if ever—come to a satisfactory conclusion on their own. **Negotiation by abstinence only allows a problem to get bigger and uglier, or it often means the opportunity goes away altogether.**

Say you did decide to act and you followed one of the concepts we just talked about. Well, at best, they would offer only short-term and ineffective ways of dealing with relationships. With these methods, negotiating is based on harming, weakening or even severing a sales/business relationship. It has nothing at all to do with creating, developing and deepening a relationship. With the latter in mind, let's look at a different kind of approach to significant sales negotiating.

People Working Together

First, we refer to our negotiation model as a **"joint venture."** Right off, you can guess that it entails fairness and parity. **A productive, motivated negotiation involves two or more parties working *together* to deal with their differences, embrace their commonalities and enhance their overall relationship.** As a matter of course, joint ventures are fair and trust is present. A negotiation looks at the situation in terms of the overall relationship. That's because differences aren't necessarily bad; often they can be complementary. If you only focus on the divisive differences, you will have tension and conflict. **If you focus on the overall relationship, you can see where differences can add up to combined strengths. If you look at a negotiation as a way of building and strengthening a relationship, you increase your chances for success tenfold**. Guaranteed.

Let's begin looking for effective ways to negotiate as a part of the relationship-enhancing process. If you think about your own career and your business relationships, some of the deepest and most solid associations involve people with whom you have had lots of experiences—both positive and challenging. I've heard many rainmakers comment on a valued relationship by saying, "*He and I have been through a lot together— both ups and downs—but he remains one of my best clients year after year. It's been great for both of us.*" Notice the words "been through a lot" and "ups and downs" in the comments. In business, just as in a marriage and in life in general, you have challenges. **How you deal with those challenges determines the strength of the overall relationship.**

Building and maintaining a healthy business relationship involves accentuating the positives and finding common ground. These things are connected and are an integral part of the relationship. Differences, then, are not "bad" (which is what most people assume when they think of a negotiation). They are simply a natural part of a relationship. Dudley Weeks, a professor of conflict resolution at the American University, defines conflict as, **"an outgrowth of the diversity that characterizes our thoughts, attitudes, beliefs, perceptions, social systems and structure."** That's a mouthful. But the important part of that definition is the word "diversity." Attitudes, beliefs and perceptions are going to differ—from person to person and from company to company. If you look at this in terms of what you can bring to the table—instead of what will keep you apart—you'll see how differences can be a positive thing.

Behavior & Workplace Motivators

It's important to think of differences in a positive light because they make up who we are. **An attitude is a viewpoint, a paradigm of thought, a way of judging or a mindset.** It is the personal filter through which we view life. Stephen Covey said this about attitudes: *"We see the world not as it is, but as we are."* Our attitudes are formed by what we hear, see, read and experience. **Your life experience forms your attitudes. Your beliefs are statements in which you have confidence.** Therefore, **a person's beliefs are important to them.** When dealing with someone in a negotiation, you have to *recognize, understand* and *focus* on what's important to the other person.

We often use an instrument that measures a person's motivators/values at work to help us define and understand how that person can do what they do better. That instrument helps us identify intensity of values in such areas as truth and knowledge, money motivation and practicality, appreciation of beauty and forms, social issues, power and position and finding meaning in life. **In a negotiation, understanding the other person's values helps you recognize what's important to *them*.** This helps you understand their point of view concerning the situation at hand. At times in our coaching business, we have had all parties involved in a significant negotiation take this assessment before we facilitate. Next, we review the results to identify key value similarities and differences. And then we have a place to start the negotiation.

We also want to stress the importance of understanding everyone's behavioral styles in a negotiation. Based on their behavioral style, people react differently in the same situation. How they act under stress differs. How they respond to a certain situation differs, based on their individual behavioral style.

Behavioral styles have the following four tendencies: First is the person's need for control and challenging activities. Second is the person's need to interact or persuade to their point of view. Third is the person's need for security and stability. Fourth is the person's need to comply with standards and their need for accuracy and cautiousness.

Do not underestimate the power of understanding a person's behavioral style. Studies show, if you don't understand and adapt your style to the other person, you will only be connecting with 25 percent to 50 percent of the people you negotiate with. Our rainmakers strive to connect with 100 percent of current and new opportunities. They do this by first understanding the different behavioral styles and, second, by adapting their behavior based on the situation.

And finally, instead of thinking of a negotiation as involving two different (and opposing) teams, visualize how the offense and defense can work together as one team to be successful. Thinking in positive terms, your goal is not to beat the other party, but, instead, to collectively work together toward a shared, mutually beneficial goal. It's a joint venture; you'll share the success.

That said, here are what we see as the necessary steps for a significant, successful negotiation:

Corsini's Guide to Effective Negotiations

1. Create an efficient, open atmosphere.
2. Clarify perceptions.
3. Focus on the needs in every relationship.
4. Build positive momentum for all parties.
5. The relationship: Past. Present. Future.
6. Brainstorm options.
7. Work out an overall, lasting and satisfying solution.
8. Monitor the success of the new solution.
9. Focus back on enhancing the overall relationship.

Now let's break it down.

1. **Create an efficient, open atmosphere.**

    Pick a time, a place, a day of the week, opening comments, etc. that are conducive to open dialogue and eventual success. For example, you might get together at a local hotel meeting room that both parties enjoy. You might meet early in the day when everyone is fresh and free of daily hassles. Finally, you might meet on a Monday, when everyone has had the weekend to recharge their emotional and physical batteries. Most people make the mistake of meeting at the office of one of the parties involved. And, more often than not, they get together at the end of a day—after the usual work-related challenges, distractions and stresses have taken their toll. From the beginning, the negotiation process will be flawed simply by the atmosphere.

    Once you decide upon an agreeable, neutral setting, make sure you are free of distractions and you have allocated enough time to talk. Turn off your phone, shut down the emails and all other distractions that block your concentration, positive energy and creativity.

    Realize **your initial comments are key to starting off on a positive note.** Remember, usually by the time you get to the negotiation, people have their guard up. You need to establish that you are interested in enhancing the overall relationship through the negotiation. It's OK and healthy to let the other party know you might agree to disagree on certain points, but make sure they understand that you are interested in deepening the overall relationship.

    A typical opening might go something like this: *"Bob, thanks for meeting me here this morning at the Ritz. I want you to know I'm not looking for some type of 'boxing match' with a winner-takes-all approach. We are in this together, so let's work together. Our relationship is important to me. We both might have some strong feelings and opinions, but I'm betting, as we put our heads together, we will come up with some fresh ideas and a positive outcome for both of us. Maybe we can't agree on everything, but I know we can come to a positive understanding that makes our overall relationship better in the long run."*

The positive atmosphere and open dialogue promote a partnership, an *esprit de corps,* and a willingness to negotiate and improve the overall business relationship. This fosters a "we-are-in-this-together" kind of attitude and not a "me-versus-you" mentality.

2. Clarify perceptions.

Perceptions are the filters through which we see ourselves, others, relationships, our company and its products and services and the day-to-day situations we encounter in business. It is imperative that you clarify the other party's perceptions and don't *assume* that your own suppositions accurately explain what each party wants out of the negotiation. The perceptions of what each party wants vary greatly from person to person. Ted Koppel said it best: *"We see the same events through different lenses. We live in the same country but different worlds."* **Never assume anything.**

Ask yourself: Am I assuming anything about the other party's wants, desires and goals? Am I reading something into the negotiation that might or might not be there?

Remember, **it's important to differentiate between needs and wants.** You'll have to figure out which points of the negotiation are about "needs" that are vital and immediate. That involves focusing on the most important "needs" within the many "wants" at hand. Think of it this way—you might want $1 million this month—and yet you need to cash flow your expenses. One is nice and optimal, and the other is urgent and needed. (In some ways you can think of this in terms of "non-negotiable" items and "negotiable" items.)

A lot of company-to-company disputes in a negotiation focus on individual wants without asking which of those goals are helping or harming the *overall relationship*. Going back to the idea of the two parties as one team, it's important to recognize that healthy, vibrant companies need long-term clients, vendors, advisors, employees, etc. in order to be successful. Looking at the negotiation in terms of a glitch in an otherwise healthy and productive long-term relationship sometimes can change the perceptions of each party.

Bottom line: You need to look authentically inward at yourself and understand what you *really* need, what your goals truly are and how you can negotiate successfully. Next, try to understand the other party's needs, wants and goals by listening without judging, if possible.

3. **Focus on the needs in every relationship.**
In any successful negotiation, the energy and focus have to be placed on the different needs operating in *every* relationship—**your needs, the other party's needs and the overall relationship's needs.** This is where a working knowledge of "internal wiring" comes into play. Taking the time to understand the other person is the first step toward shared success. Think about the other party's behavioral style and workplace motivators and how they express these things.

Based on their behavioral style, try to understand their need to control a situation; their desire to persuade you to their point of view; their need to help others, their motivation for security and stability; and finally, their need to comply with standards and maintain accuracy.

Next, understand what motivates you in the negotiation by understanding your workplace motivators and what values the other party has at work. Remember, the six values that drive people are theoretical, utilitarian, aesthetic, social, individualistic and traditional. People with high theoretical values love knowledge, ideas and exploring. High utilitarians desire wealth and expect a return on investment of time, energy and money. High aesthetic people place value on form and function—like the arts, gardening, interior design, etc. Social people value helping others like the poor or doing social work. Individualists value winning and power. And finally, high traditionalists value living by a set of rules and encourage others to accept those same values. Many people equate this to religion, but it applies to conservatism.

In any negotiation, you must determine if *your* needs are being met or being ignored. Are you satisfied with the relationship? Does the negotiation seem fair to you? Is the proposed outcome reflective of your values? These questions help you **understand if you have a needs issue; whether or not there are significant misconceptions; or if the negotiation involves worthwhile and shared goals, values,** etc. Ask yourself: Is the other party aware of my needs? You might want to better communicate your needs and offer a clear action plan that can help fulfill those needs.

Next, focus on the other party's needs. Do you have a clear understanding of those needs? What do they need from the relationship that you might not be giving? **Remember to think in terms of your overall relationship as you listen closely to the other party's needs.**

Now you are ready to focus on the needs of the overall relationship. What might, at first, look like a critical need of an individual might be discounted or minor when looking at the big picture or overall relationship. Simply put, **a need that initially satisfies you might not be that important in the context of the bigger picture and a long-term relationship.** The overall relationship becomes the reason for successful negotiation—not the initial points.

Once you have addressed your needs, the other party's needs and the overall relationship's needs, **you have the foundation for a successful negotiation**—and a stronger, deeper relationship.

One word of caution: You might do everything right and still not come to a satisfactory conclusion in your negotiation. That's because this action doesn't exist in a vacuum. There might be relationships or factors outside the room—and your negotiation efforts—that have influence over the outcome.

You could do an effective job of clarifying your needs, understanding the other party's needs and attending to the needs of the overall relationship. Yet, there could be another relationship outside of the negotiation with sway. For instance, the company CEO might favor a competitor, for a variety of reasons. You could do everything right, and yet that relationship outside of the room could ultimately overshadow everything you are working toward. This is why we challenge people to maintain multiple opportunities in their Best Bets™ Opportunities Pipeline and live and work according to the abundance principle. Sometimes business isn't fair. But if you're prepared, you can simply regard the negotiation as valuable experience and move on to other opportunities.

4. **Build positive momentum for all parties.**

In any negotiation, you have positives and negatives. That's where the compromise comes in! But there's no need for negative energy. **It is up to each party to focus their energy and creativity on the positives.** At least one person has to focus on the positives and make certain to use the energy of the negotiation to move forward. Be that person! Encourage the other party to use positive energy to look for solutions, too. If you keep reaching, eventually they come.

One of the most dramatic examples of the power of positive energy on a negative situation involved a Christian prison ministry called Kairos, which I was involved with several years ago. We worked in a maximum-security facility with many inmates who were serving life sentences without parole. They faced a bleak situation. Many were in their early 20's. On a typical four-day weekend retreat we spent with them, the inmates invariably began the weekend angry, detached and disinterested. All during the weekend, we continuously encouraged them by showering them with love and attention in a non-judgmental way. We encouraged them to open up about their feelings. By the fourth day, most of the inmates were smiling, engaged and clearly affected by our efforts. I contribute this transformation to positive Christian energy. Talk about positive momentum!

Now if we were able to create positive momentum with men who were in an undeniably grim situation, certainly you can create positive energy in your business negotiations.

5.   The relationship: Past. Present. Future.

Every meaningful relationship has a past; present; and, managed correctly, a future. The negotiation involves all three. Sometimes starting with the past (or even the present) bogs down both parties or involves too much negativity. Looking forward can create a positive, hopeful environment for improving past and current behaviors. This view is one of better tomorrows (an important part of the abundance principle). **It focuses the attention on what can be done now and in the future, no matter what has happened in the past or is going on in the present**. If you can find a couple of positive steps with which to proceed, then you can use that momentum to move the entire negotiation forward.

But consider this: Sometimes by looking at the past, you can find common ground. Perhaps you can identify past positive experiences. Talk about how you both got together initially. Remember how you effectively worked together on a successful project in the past. Then, remembering the good things, you might want to explore your differences. **Learn from the past, acknowledge the present and focus on a shared vision for the future**.

6. Brainstorm options.

You came into the negotiation with some predetermined options and so did the other party or parties. Now that you have laid the foundation for mutual success, focus your attention on generating new options, new solutions, and new ways of resolving the negotiation and enhancing the overall relationship. Brainstorm. Challenge each other to come up with mutually beneficial ideas. (Notice that ideas is plural. Create options.)

Before using this model of negotiation, you might have been inwardly focused and perhaps even mentally blocked from moving forward together. **With this shared positive energy and a real understanding of individual and shared needs, you now are ready to explore new and exciting shared solutions.** Work together as you brainstorm these options, and write them down as quickly as you think of them.

7. Work out an overall, lasting and satisfying solution.

After brainstorming options to complete the negotiation, it's now time to reach an agreement on an overall solution. This is when you address the finer points in the negotiation. Seek a positive result by working on the finer points with the overall (and now-agreed-upon) ultimate solution in mind. Remember, this is still part of the negotiation process (perhaps the hardest part), and you both are still moving forward to a deeper relationship and a satisfying final solution. **It is imperative for both parties to be involved and mutually benefited; trust and confidence must be gained and maintained.** Without trust and a mutually beneficial outcome, one or both parties might fall back into their previous positions.

Keep this in mind at this point in the negotiation: Don't attempt to tackle major differences until you have experienced some new successes in the negotiation process. You're not there until you're really there.

Also, make sure you are not just coming up with a quick fix or temporary solution to the problem at hand. **That is why both parties must be involved in the development of viable options. Look long-term. Act with the big picture in mind. Work toward solutions that are both mutually beneficial and long-lasting.**

Continue to work toward an overall solution, addressing all the final, finer points. You have positive momentum going for you. Use it to come to closure on the negotiation.

Before you know it, your negotiation is finished.

8. **Monitor the success of the new solution.**

So you've completed the negotiation, and it's a win-win for both parties. You worked hard using the truth, positive energy and understanding. You acted in a sprit of fairness. The result mutually benefits both parties. Congratulations! The negotiation is over, but your work is not. Now it's time for both parties to deliver what they promised and agreed upon. You approached the negotiation from a standpoint of abundance—and you both ultimately got what you wanted. Now you need to move forward in that same mindset.

Delivering what you promised is critical—plus it's the right and authentic thing to do. Monitor your progress. Come through. Do what you said you were going to do—and then, perhaps, do more.

9. **Focus back on enhancing the overall relationship.**

The reason you decided to negotiate at all is because you value your relationship. Otherwise, why bother? Enhance and strengthen this relationship by focusing your time, talents and resources on making it better. A significant negotiation takes a lot of energy and effort. Chances are, your "emotional batteries" could stand to be recharged. Consider a meal at a restaurant you both like, go hunting, go fishing, whatever. Just do something that will focus on the relationship and remind you both of why you made the effort to negotiate in the first place.

Sample Negotiation

Each and every negotiation is different because each one is influenced by various skills, attitudes and style. There is no absolute right way to negotiate. The guidelines we've discussed, however, can make your efforts more effective and enjoyable. Yes, enjoyable. We often look at negotiating as unpleasant, because it involves differences and conflict, but negotiating need not be characterized by bad feelings or angry behavior. To bring together the concepts we've discussed and to show that negotiation can be a positive experience, let's look at a hypothetical negotiation situation:

Please note, this sample negotiation takes place during several conversations over a period of time.

1. Create an efficient, open atmosphere.

You: "Susan, thank you for meeting with me today at the Summit Club; the view from up here is spectacular, and the food is good, too. I think it's a great place for a discussion. When we talked on the phone the other day, you said that you were going to ask some other insurance agents to quote your insurance since you haven't evaluated other proposals in five years. Well, I want you to know I'm not going to try to put a guilt trip on you for wanting to do that. I understand that business is business. You and I have been working together for these past five years, and we have been through a lot—some of it good, some of it challenging. I value you, and I appreciate your business. That's why I want us to talk today. Let's see where the conversation takes us."

Susan: "That sounds like a fine and fair idea. But I want you to know up front we want to talk to other agents. "

2. Clarify perceptions.

You: "As the CFO, I know your job—or better said, your responsibility—is to be the financial steward for the company. I've always admired how capably you look after the company's well being. Bob has always depended on you for that, and I know this involves getting the best deal on your insurance. Without me assuming, what is the thinking for getting other proposals?"

Susan: "Bob and I talked in our last executive board meeting, and we realized that it has been a long time since we reviewed our insurance programs. With the economy tightening and our banker looking closely at our financials, we want to make sure we are saving money and reducing costs wherever possible. As Bob said, 'It doesn't hurt checking the market to make sure we are paying the least we can for insurance.'"

You: "Obviously, I don't blame you for wanting to save money. There is a reason your company has thrived for over 50 years; you don't get to be as good as you are in your industry by chance. Other than reducing costs, is there any other reason you are going out into the market? Please be authentic with me."

Susan: "No, you and your agency have done a great job. We just want to make sure we are getting the lowest price possible for insurance."

You: "Susan, that certainly helps me understand your motivation. Based on the annual client surveys you've filled out over the past two years, you told us you were very satisfied with our efforts to help you manage your risks and ultimately keep down the cost of your insurance. Since we are having this conversation, something has changed. Please elaborate."

Susan: "It just comes down to dollars and cents..."

3. Focus on the needs in every relationship.

You: "I hear you saying you want the lowest price for insurance, and that's fair. You and I have talked about my philosophy on our business relationship—I want to continue to be your insurance and risk-management *advisor*. I consider your success to be my success as well. I feel we're a team, and our relationship is based on truth and fairness and is certainly mutually beneficial. I do value that. What are your thoughts on our business relationship?"

Susan: "You know I appreciate what you have done for us over the years. You have worked in an advisory role, and that means a lot..."

You: "You've been in business a long time, and you and I both know that major change is disruptive and often takes a lot of energy and time. Remember what we went through two years ago when you agreed with my recommendation to switch carriers? You ended up with a much better program for just a little more money, but it took some work. What would it cost you in time and resources if you changed agencies *and* started with a new carrier?"

Susan: "I hate to even think about what it would take to start all over with two new relationships. But for the right savings, we might be forced to change. We are looking to improve our returns on investments as well as our bottom line. Of course, we need vendors like you who we can count on to have our best interests at heart. I feel like I'm in a 'push-pull' situation right now."

You: "I hear you loud and clear; improving your bottom line i[s] important. And I don't want to pressure you. In fact, I won't But let's keep talking and see where we end up ..."

4. Build positive momentum for all parties.

You: "Think back for a moment to last year when you ha[d] that fire in the restroom of your call center. There wasn't muc[h] fire damage, but the smoke damage was significant."

Susan: "Oh yes, I remember. We were lucky it happene[d] during the shift change and nobody was hurt—or ever worse. I appreciate your being on site within two hours o[f] that fire."

You: "I came as quickly as possible. If the shoe were on the other foot, I would have wanted my agent to be there righ[t] away. Of course, prompt follow-up was important, too. That'[s] why when we first started working together I asked you t[o] put my personal contact information in your cell phone."

Susan: "I remember when you asked me to do that—I mus[t] say, initially, I was surprised by your request."

You: "Remember how Allen, our agency claims person, wa[s] all over the carrier the next morning to cut you a check righ[t] away so you could begin the clean-up? We understood tha[t] every moment the call center was down was costing yo[u] time and money. We were very sensitive to that point. We had to get you up and running again. I'm happy we were able to come through for you in your time of need."

5. The relationship: Past. Present. Future.

You: "You know, the more we talk, the more I'm reminde[d] about what we've been through during the past five years. Remember three years ago when you made the acquisitio[n] in Atlanta? You and I worked hard to consolidate all o[f] their coverages into your current policies. We knew tha[t] consolidating the coverages would save you money ove[r] having separate policies."

Susan: "Yes, I remember. It took us 18 months to negotiate the deal, and we only had three days to convert them ove[r] to our policies. I appreciated your help."

You: "We'll always be there for you and your company. As I said, your success is our success. Let's continue ou[r] discussion . . ."

Brainstorm options.

You: "Susan, as an agency, part of our job is to take your insurance out to the marketplace and make sure *you* are getting the very best value. We do that every year. I also feel a personal responsibility to you and Bob to make sure we are taking care of you. But price is only one part of the risk-management game."

Susan (somewhat jokingly): "You aren't going to give me the risk-management talk again, are you?"

You: "Yes, I am. I raise that topic because if you are really serious about saving money, I have a better idea. Let's focus on what you and I can do *together* to reduce your company's risks because that will, in turn, save you money..."

Work out an overall, lasting and satisfying solution.

You: "As we discussed several times in the past, we have various initiatives at the agency directed at helping our clients reduce their risk. With so many female clerical employees in your call centers, you, like most companies in your line of work, have an increased exposure for sexual harassment—especially since 68 percent of your supervisors are male. I'd like for us to look at the anti-harassment training proposal I gave you six months ago at our mid-year 'How are we doing?' session. When you reduce your risks, you can save money..."

Susan: "OK, OK. I get the picture. I'm going to go back to Bob and remind him of all the things we've accomplished together and how you've helped us save money over the past five years. And I'm going to recommend to him we conduct the supervisory training you suggested..."

You: "Great."

Susan: "I can't promise you we won't meet with other brokers, but I am going to revisit this with Bob and I'll call you next week."

You: "OK. I would love to talk with the two of you together after you meet…"

(Two weeks later after the advisory salesperson met with Susan and Bob, they decided to stay with their agent, conduct the training with their supervisors and renew their policies.)

8. **Monitor the success of the new solution.**

   (Three months later.)

   You: "Susan, it's been a month since your renewal. How do you think it went? Your company is better because of the supervisory training your people went through. Over time, you will save money by avoiding or reducing any harassment claims and complaints. What else can we do for you?"

9. **Focus back on enhancing the overall relationship.**

   You: "Mary and I would like to take you and Charles to Ocean next week for dinner. Is Ocean still your favorite restaurant? Look at your schedule, and let us know what evening works best for you. We can just spend the time enjoying each other's company. I'm looking forward to that."

Reference Points

"Selling through referrals is the most effective and efficient way to grow your business."
— Marc Corsini

INSIDE

Reference Points Overview

Good References: Corsini's Guide To a Successful Referral System

There is nothing more fundamental about the sales process than an effective referral system. Nothing. Nada. Zip. This is how you grow your business.

As we have said, we've been fortunate to work with some of the top rainmakers in the United States. And over the years, our research shows that even these rainmakers with their high degrees of skill and years of proven success don't take full advantage of the No. 1 selling tool available to them—referrals. They don't ask for, obtain and then follow up with referrals on a regular basis. In fact, fewer than 3 percent of the people we coach use this powerful tool as much as they should. And it's costing them additional relationships, sales, income, profits and precious selling time.

In this chapter, we'll explain exactly why referrals are so important. Then we'll show you the best ways to go about getting them. We see it as a four-part system:

1. **Understand the referral process.**
2. **Ask for and obtain referrals.**
3. **Follow up promptly with those referrals.**
4. **Repeat the process every working day.**

Understanding the referral process means realizing the value of being proactive. You are creating your own Best Bets™ Opportunities. We encourage you to live a life of abundance and recognize that opportunities to succeed and grow your business are everywhere. So, too, are prospects to improve your life (in and out of the office), enhance your relationships (business and personal) and simply be happier. But although these opportunities are out there, they don't always come directly to you. You have to be proactive and take charge of your own success. One thing leads to others in the referral process.

To make the referral process work, you must be wiling to ask for and obtain referrals. This might be something you are unaccustomed to doing. As you'll see on the following pages, we're not asking you to do something that will make you inordinately uncomfortable. You will be approaching friends, family and people you work with closely. These are people who want you to succeed, and so they should be willing to help you.

You must follow up on the referrals you receive and do this promptly. Otherwise, your requests are a wasted effort. Get into the habit of obtaining the referral and then acting quickly.

Finally, a successful referral system depends on your repeating the process every day. You'll need to do this even when you're enjoying an abundance of business. Regular requests for referrals will keep you sharp and focused on your success. Plus, as with just about any endeavor, the more you practice, the better you become.

To help you make the most of this effective and essential business tool, you'll find an article in this chapter titled **Good References: Corsini's Guide To a Successful Referral System**. It features 20 smart, practical tips you can put to work immediately to start obtaining referrals today.

If you follow our advice in this chapter, faithfully document your referrals and then follow up on them, success will come. That's because the information here will help you work smarter. It will help you Do What You Do Better.

Reference Points Overview

For most people, business development is usually a "new relationship" type of activity. You are trying to grow your business by establishing new Best Bets™ Opportunities through new clients. Simply put: **The more relationships you have, the greater your potential for success.** The fewer relationships you have, the less chance you have for growing your business and achieving your goals—never mind overachieving.

It's all about increasing your "center of influence" where one contact leads to others. Business development involves adding to the number of people in this important network. This happens when current relationships lead you to new business connections—and profitable new business.

Traditional models for adding new relationships (and growing your center of influence) include:

1. Telephone prospecting time (your daily "Hour of Power")
2. Mass marketing (a combination of media including emails, traditional post office mailings, newsletters, personal notes, novelty items with your company's name on them, etc.)
3. Trade shows/chamber meetings/social clubs, etc.
4. Advertising (electronic and print)
5. Good, old-fashioned "knocking on doors"

Now all these activities work just fine. And we're all for them—to a point. But there is a more effective and efficient way to grow your business.

The thing is, these aforementioned activities, and others like them, normally involve a whole lot of action taken in *anticipation* of producing the desired results. Mind you, there is nothing terribly detrimental about this approach to selling. It is the traditional way of business solicitation for a great many people. The downside is that it takes an enormous amount of effort, money and time (and some level of frustration) to produce profitable results. In many ways, the return often doesn't justify the effort. The pain-to-gain ratio doesn't add up for most people, and that's why they don't grow their businesses as much and as quickly as they should on a yearly basis.

But as we said, there's an easier, more effective way to get the results you want and need.

By asking for, obtaining and following up with a referral, you are bypassing all of the traditional sales steps to establishing a new relationship. **If someone gives you a referral, they essentially are giving you an *endorsement*. They are validating you and your work by allowing you to use their name in reference.** And the trust, respect and admiration they have for you can get a new business relationship off to a very good and solid start.

To illustrate this point, let's consider two very different strategies for approaching the same new-business opportunity.

Let's first look at the typical way most people go about selling:

Let's say you work for a company that designs Websites for businesses. You, just like everyone else in your field, want to increase your business by adding new clients. So you decide to send out a packet of information to Carol Walls, the president of a large construction company. You have identified this company as a potential client; it is in your Best Bet's™ Pipeline of opportunities. You work with lots of contractors, and you know you can help this company develop a better Website and increase its *own* business.

A couple of workdays after you've mailed the information to Ms. Walls, you call her to arrange a face-to-face appointment. When you finally reach her (you've probably played a bit of phone tag by now, and you've had to make your way past the assistant or telephone receptionist), you tell her your name, the name of your company and that your company designs Websites for contractors.

Ms. Walls *might* take the time to listen to this much of what you have to say. But you're more than likely going to get a *"Thanks, but no thanks—we already have a Website"* response.

Now let's say you take a different, more targeted and personal approach. Rather than begin your prospecting efforts by sending out a packet of information, you first call around to several people you know and work with (this is your "center of influence") to see if any of them know Ms. Walls. It turns out that Richard Goodman (one of your best clients and known as "Rick" to those close to him) happens to go to church with Ms. Walls. What's more, they are in the church's Wednesday Night Supper Club together. Rick agrees to call and tell his friend Carol about how much he admires and trusts you, how great your company is and that he thinks you can help her grow her own business with a more exciting and more easily navigated Website. Now let's replay the call.

You: "Ms. Walls, this is Mark Sites. Rick Goodman gave me your name and suggested I call you."

Her: "I saw Rick on Wednesday night; he sure thinks the world of you."

You (humbly): "Thanks very much, Ms. Walls."

Her: "Call me 'Carol.'"

You: "Thank you, Carol. Now I know you're busy, but I hoped I could come by for 20 minutes sometime next week and talk about how your company's Website can help you attract new business."

Her: "I'm not sure we are interested; we already have a Website."

You: "Yes, I've been to your Website. It's good, but I believe we can make it better. All of our clients already had Websites when we first started working with them, but each of them has seen increased traffic and more clients after we made their sites more interesting and easier to access. But we can talk more about that when we get together."

Her: "OK. I'll give you those 20 minutes. Let's say Tuesday at 10 a.m."

You: "Great. I'll see you then. I'm looking forward to showing you how we can help you do what you do better."

As you can see, a personal connection (achieved with a simple referral) puts an entirely different spin on the same type of sales call. The referral-aided call allows you to immediately establish a connection. It opens up the door for a faster and deeper relationship—one that would have taken months to develop with traditional business-building activities.

Now Ms. Walls might or might not be a current Best Bets™ and buy from you this year. But even if she doesn't, your efforts yielded favorable results and a Future Best Bets™ Opportunity. What has happened is that you, with very little time and effort, have expanded your center of influence. And with that expansion, new business will follow over time.

Why Not Just Ask?

So if getting referrals is such a powerful business-building tool, why don't people do it more often? Well, we think it's because while **asking for referrals is easy to do, it's just as easy *not* to do.**

Think about it. If you don't ask for referrals, nothing different or terribly bad happens in your day. There are no immediate consequences. Your spouse generally does not ask you at the end of the day: *"Honey, how many referrals did you get today?"* or *"Did you call the two referrals you received yesterday?"*

On the other hand, she, your boss, other salespeople and even perhaps your children often will ask you: *"Did you sell anything today?"*

It's little wonder then, that we tend to focus on the immediate action (and gratification) of closing the sale. And we don't bother to ask for and obtain referrals that will pay off in the future.

As we've shown, that's not the way to build your business and increase your sales. The information on the next several pages will help you get in the habit of asking for (and utilizing) referrals. **Good References: Corsini's Guide To a Successful Referral System** is a list of 20 highly effective and workable tips to help you better develop your own profitable referral system and keep your pipeline full of current and future opportunities. Read these tips, and implement them. Then keep track of your efforts. Begin today, and you'll Do What You Do Better.

Good References: Corsini's Guide To a Successful Referral System

1. Ask and you shall receive.

Sounds simple, and it is. But most people don't bother to ask for referrals. Therefore, they are unable to take advantage of this obvious and powerful business–development tool. Ask. And ask often.

2. If nobody gives you referrals, something ain't right.

If you're asking for referrals but you're not getting them, then you should find out why. You might have customer–satisfaction difficulties or perception problems you need to address. Ask those clients, with whom you have a deep and authentic relationship, why they are hesitant to give you a referral. Consider sending out a client survey to figure out what's going on. There are several good Web-based surveying companies, and the investment is low. Solve any problems that exist, and then start asking again.

3. Be specific.

When salespeople finally do ask for referrals, they generally say: *"Do you know of someone I should call?"* Their clients often respond: *"Let me think about it, and I will let you know."* And that's the end of it. Help your clients help you. Be specific. Guide them to an answer you can use. Describe your ideal Best Bets™ Opportunities and your optimal client. Give them something to go on.

4. Keep asking.

Most people treat referral campaigns like the health club in January. They are fired up when they first begin, and then they start to slack off. **Continuing to ask for and obtain**

referrals is the most important rule. Collecting referrals, like being fit, is not a one-time exercise. It's a long-term (and career-long) practice.

5. **Keep score.**

   Track your progress. Use an organized system as an accountability tool to keep track of how many referrals you are getting on a monthly basis and the status of those referrals. Hold yourself accountable to someone about the number of referrals you plan to pursue each month and whether or not you consistently reach your goals.

6. **All referrals are not created (valued) equal.**

   Some referrals are more valuable than others. And sometimes it's a matter of timing. Prioritize prospective clients according to time of year, level of importance, their centers of influence, how well you know them, etc. For example, if someone refers you to a CPA during tax season, don't try to set up an appointment to talk about how you can help him or her until after crunch time. Timing can be everything.

   And remember, successful people usually spend time with other successful people; CEOs hang with other CEOs. So the quality of a referral often is based on the person who gives it to you.

7. **Establish your "Go-To Group."**

   This will be your primary network of referral sources. Make a list of people who think you "hung the moon." These are people with whom you enjoy a strong, meaningful relationship. These people want to see you succeed. They care about you and your success. They probably know lots of other people, too. Use this center of influence as a starting point to begin accumulating referrals. These are your best clients, closest friends and business associates, people you've helped over the years, etc. Think big; this list could include your minister or rabbi, former Boy or Girl Scout leader, someone you serve with on a civic or volunteer board, etc. Start your referral search with this group, and go back to them periodically for additional referrals.

8. **Identify your "Go-To-Next Group."**

   Consider this to be your secondary network of referrals. These are businesspeople and other acquaintances you know (maybe some even casually) who are willing to help you. They have a center of influence that includes lots of people, but you need to further develop a relationship with *them* (and gain their trust) so that they will feel comfortable referring you to others. While we call them your "Go-To-Next Group," you should follow up with these people at the same time you're working with your "Go-To Group." This list will take more time to develop, so begin today.

9. Ask for referrals in writing.

Do not assume you always have to verbally ask for a referral. Consider sending a one-page letter requesting referrals. Mark Sheer, a referral guru, suggests using phrases like, *"I'm expanding my business, and I need your help. Who do you know ..."* And then you provide a specific profile of the particular kind of ideal Best Bets™ Opportunities you're after. He suggests asking for at least three names.

10. Look to unusual sources for referrals.

Include in your referral source list association executives, editors, chamber of commerce people, industry groups and people who sell to you. People who sell to you are a tremendous source of referrals. They certainly have a vested interest in your success—they want you to succeed because they want to grow *their* business.

11. Get 'em before you need 'em.

Most people stop asking for referrals when they get busy and have a backlog of Best Bets™ Opportunities. The best time to build a solid foundation of referrals is when you do *not* need the business. If you wait until you need the business, it will be too late. Referrals obtained today generally pay off in the future, and we're not talking about within a month. Remember, Noah built the ark *before* it was raining.

12. Your competition can be a referral source.

Do not think of your competition as "the enemy" all the time. In many fields, a portion of new business comes when the competition does not have the expertise or time to solve a client's problem. Working jointly on projects often leads to referrals, too. Let your competition know you are open to opportunities that are a win-win situation for both parties. Trust and respect are key to the success and cooperation between any groups.

13. **Ask for advice instead of a referral.**

When calling someone for a referral, consider asking for advice instead. Even if you want referrals from them, say: *"What would you do if you were me and you wanted to grow your business?"* They might lead you to additional referral sources, give actual referrals or offer some great advice on how to do what you do better. Make sure to be authentic when asking for someone's advice. And listen carefully. People can always tell if you are genuinely interested in what they have to share.

14. **Send thank-you notes.**

When someone gives you a referral, send that person a handwritten note thanking them for the name(s). If the referral becomes a client, call the referral source and give them the good news. If it's a big enough deal, consider sending the referral source a small thank-you gift. Do not, however, give the appearance of buying help or paying them off.

15. **Explain what you do.**

Send new referrals a letter, CD, video, or direct them to a Website, and then candidly discuss how you have helped other people. It would be great if you could include a client testimonial or a letter of recommendation, too.

16. **The message matters.**

This is key. What you first say when you call the referral is very important. Establish your connection immediately. Use a phrase like this one: *"Isabella Wold asked me to call you because she thought you might benefit from some of the same things we did for her company..."*

17. **Have confidence when you call or meet someone.**

You only get one chance to make a first impression, so make the most of it. Everyone is busy today. Your presence should reinforce your professionalism, confidence and ability to help.

18. **Timely follow-up is critical after calling.**

Often people will tell you that now is not a good time for them to talk or meet, and they will ask you to send them information and call back in a couple of weeks. Make sure you have the ability and materials to do this. Follow up with a timely email, letter, informative e-newsletter, etc. *the same day* you initially call someone. Next, schedule a follow-up (by phone or, better yet, face to face) in whatever contact manager you use.

19. Have fun, but expect rejection.

Do not let any lack of excitement on behalf of the person you are calling lower your own energy level. People get lots of calls and emails; you can't realistically expect them to be eager to talk to you. Use your positive energy level to capture their interest and turn your call into a positive one.

20. Start today, and remember it's an "everyday thing."

Obtaining referrals is a lot like exercising. If you do it regularly, you will get stronger. Then you'll be able to accomplish more and build an abundant pipeline of Best Bets™ Opportunities. If you don't, you become weak. Even the easiest tasks become difficult, and you'll be looking at a life of scarcity. Focus on obtaining useful referrals, and then put them to work. That's how you live a life of abundance with opportunities everywhere—they are yours for the asking.

Produce Results

"Rainmakers have an abundance mentality. They see opportunities in everything they do."
— Marc Corsini

INSIDE

Abundant Living and the 80/20 Principle

Rainmaker Productivity Test

**An Abundance of Workable Tips
(and Some Commonsense Sayings)**

Successful people know that in work—and in life—there is opportunity everywhere. We call this an "abundance mentality," and in this chapter, we'll explore how it applies to your day-to-day productivity and your long-term goals of reaching your potential as a salesperson. Please don't think the abundance principle is some type of "new age" mumbo-jumbo. It's not. It is, however, a positive attitude toward life that all winners share.

The abundance principle is based on living life to the fullest. It is nurtured when you *expect* success to result from your efforts. In this chapter, we're going to take this concept and expand it to your Best Bets™ Opportunity Pipeline. We'll look at how it applies to time management and being as productive as possible. And all the while, we'll keep in mind a steady focus on **The 7 F's of *True* Success**. That's because the abundance principle doesn't just apply at work—it touches all aspects of your life.

People either live and function in a place of abundance or a place of scarcity. Rainmakers approach what they do from an abundant-life perspective. They see opportunities everywhere, and they work to make them pay off. They work smarter rather than harder. They expect to succeed, and they work toward specific goals in order to make that happen. They think strategically, develop a plan, and they work that plan in an optimistic, deliberate way.

Underachievers, on the other hand, come at work (and sometimes at life) with a scarcity mentality. Often they function in a haphazard and lackadaisical way. Success with a scarcity mentality depends on a vibrant economy, the perfect product mix and a 95 percent Best Bets™ Pipeline win rate year after year. In short, it depends on luck. This is why those salespeople with a scarcity mentality usually have a yo-yo history to their performance efforts. They range from good to bad and perhaps back to bad again year after year. A rainmaker's performance record just gets steadily better—going from good to great and then even greater from one year to the next.

Someone working under the scarcity model might have a day like this: They're at work, and around 10:20 a.m. they look up and realize suddenly how little they've accomplished. Then they wonder, "Where has the morning gone?" They've been busy enough, but they've gotten very little done. It's kind of like that movie *Groundhog Day* when Bill Murray is forced to live the same day over and over until he gets it right. Unfortunately, a scarcity mentality—with insufficient planning, a less-than-positive outlook and little focus—doesn't often result in getting it right.

In general, most rainmakers know exactly where their time goes. The day isn't scripted for them, but they do approach it (and work it) with deliberation and with focus.

If you already work with an abundance mentality, good for you! Keep it up. (You will, because you know it works.) If you have more of a scarcity mentality, let's work on that. And know this: You *can* become more effective and productive. It's a matter of pinpointing how you spend your day, overcoming time-wasting hurdles and focusing on the **Fundamentals of Selling**. An abundance perspective enhances your productivity, and that translates into more Best Bets™ Opportunities in your pipeline. Your daily "hour of power" contact time becomes easier to accomplish and more rewarding. You'll have more face-to-face visits, deeper relationships with the clients you currently have and you'll find that more deals come to fruition. Ultimately, you'll discover true success—in and out of your office because a hopeful, positive outlook affects all areas of your life.

As you read this chapter, we encourage you to reflect on how you spend each day. Coming to a true realization of how effectively and efficiently you work allows you to see whether or not your time and talents are really being used in a productive manner. You'll need to check your attitude, too, and work to develop a mind-set of abundance.

Our ideas on the abundance principle and productivity (and consequently, your performance) are based on our proven sales coaching methods as well as our experience working with thousands of talented individuals at hundreds of companies all across the United States. While coaching some of the top rainmakers in the country, we've seen what works—and what doesn't. We'll share some of those sales dos and don'ts here.

But first, we'll offer you a step-by-step guide to realizing just how productive you really are. With **Abundant Living and the 80/20 Principle** that we talked about earlier, we'll look at the classic and highly successful (and true) **80/20 Principle** and how it applies to what you do. Salespeople at any level can utilize the many applications of this smart approach to work.

Then there's our **Rainmaker Productivity Test**. Take it, and quickly see just how effective and efficient you are at work.

Finally, we offer **An Abundance of Workable Tips (and Some Commonsense Sayings)**. These words of wisdom and proven ideas on productivity and time management are here to make you think (and perhaps even grin a little). Read them with the abundance principle in mind. Then get out there and Do What You Do Better.

Abundant Living and the 80/20 Principle

To get the most from the abundance mentality way of life, it's important to approach this from a sensible standpoint: Not all opportunities are alike. That's where the **80/20 Principle** comes in. And in this chapter we are going to explore the principle in more detail. It's one thing to live and work with a positive, winning attitude; it's another to function in a smart, discerning way—knowing just where you need to focus that positive energy.

The 80/20 Principle states that 80 percent of the results, outputs or rewards are derived from only 20 percent of the causes, inputs or efforts. Simply stated, only a few major things make up the majority of any success. This idea has a multitude of applications for all salespeople.

Vilfredo Pareto (1848-1932), an Italian economist, studied the pattern of wealth and income in 19th-century England. In 1897, he found that most income and wealth went to a minority. For example, his logic was that if 20 percent of the population enjoyed 80 percent of the wealth, then you could reliably predict that 10 percent would have 65 percent of the wealth and 5 percent would have 50 percent and so on.

While he was onto something, Pareto never really used his 80/20 formula in any practical way. Eventually, he moved on to other research, and his findings were forgotten until the late 1940s.

In 1949, a Harvard professor named George K. Zipf came up with the "**Principle of Least Effort**." Zipf's principle said that resources (people, goods, time, skills or anything else that is productive) tend to arrange themselves so as to minimize work, and that approximately 20 to 30 percent of any resource accounts for 70 to 80 percent of the activity related to that resource.

But it wasn't until 1951 when Romanian-born Joseph Moses Juran, a quality-control guru and U.S. engineer, published the *Quality Control Handbook* citing Pareto's 80/20 Principle. Juran's concept used the 80/20 Principle to root out quality faults and improve the reliability and value of industrial and consumer goods. Juran's theories were not initially embraced by U.S. industries. But starting in 1953, while working with several Japanese corporations, he is credited with transforming the value and quality of their consumer goods. It wasn't until the early 1970s that he brought his quality model to the U.S.

These great minds call this theory by different names and approach the idea from various angles, but they all agree on this: Some opportunities are more lucrative, rewarding, fun, worthwhile, etc. than others. So thinking in terms of your time and productivity and coming at this with an abundance mentality, let's figure out how you should spend 80 percent of your time, talents and resources. We'll look at the 80/20 Principle in relation to several aspects of your business life.

The 80/20 Principle certainly applies to current clients and current and future Best Bets™ Opportunities. We all know there are lucrative clients and then there are those who prove to be a waste of time. Applying Pareto's principle, we find that **20 percent of your clients will generate 80 percent of your revenue and income**. So, according to the **80/20 Client Principle**, the **majority of your time should be spent with a few specific clients and potential clients.**

Understanding and recognizing which clients generate the most revenue/profits allows you to better decide how to structure and schedule your face-to-face sales calls and who to call during your "hour of power." Commit to focusing on the right Best Bets™ Opportunities, and let someone else have the rest!

Next let's apply the 80/20 Principle to your productivity. From this standpoint, we see that **20 percent of your time, talents and activities generates 80 percent of your revenue and income**. The challenge with the **80/20 Productivity Principle** is to clearly identify which of your many daily activities are actually helping to generate that revenue and income. From our sales-coaching experience, we've established that the following activities generate an inordinate amount of revenue and income. No matter how you look at it, you'll do well to spend time doing these things:

- **Build solid relationships.** Spend most of your time, talents and resources with quality clients and potential opportunities that you know have a future with you. These relationships are based on trust, respect and admiration by both parties—and they are mutually beneficial. That's how you recognize them.

- **Focus on your best opportunities**. Best Bets™ Opportunities look like your best clients. They want and need what you're offering—just like your current best clients do. These are the opportunities that will ultimately generate 80 percent of your income. Identify them, and then spend most of your time nurturing them.

- **Be an advisor to your clients.** You should be more than just a supplier of goods or services. Be a partner in your clients' success. Work to gain and maintain their trust. Act with *their* best interests in mind. With commitment and absolute authenticity on your part, you'll become as trusted an advisor to your clients as their CPAs and attorneys.

- **Solve problems for clients and potential clients**. Make yourself indispensable to your best clients and your most promising opportunities. Put yourself in their shoes, and approach what you do from their company's perspective. What problems do they face? How can you help them solve those problems? Make their issues your issues, and you both profit.

- **Identify market changes, and then act.** Constantly look for better ways to do what you do better. Be proactive in your efforts rather than just reactive. Embrace change, and put it to work for you.

- **Delegate**. Let others work hard while you work smart. Again, focus your time and talents in the most effective way possible. Concentrate on that rewarding 20 percent.

- **Simplify your life**. More is not necessarily better. Sometimes it's just bigger, takes additional effort and burns up your energy. Figure out what's really important to you, and focus your time, talents and energy there. Think of this in terms of life outside the office, too. It impacts each of **The 7 F's of *True* Success**.

Now let's apply the 80/20 Principle to your decision-making process. **The *80/20 Decision-Making Principle* states that only 20 percent of your decisions are really important.** So don't sweat every decision that comes your way. Focus your main energy on the few really crucial decisions that you *have* to make. Just work through the others, and move on. Or better yet, delegate them.

The 80/20 Principle even applies to days of the week. The **80/20 Productive Days Principle states that only 20 percent of your workweek generates 80 percent of your revenue.** Which days are most productive for you? Do you start each week with focus and determination? Do you work up to a big finish by week's end? Is the middle of the week when you hit your stride? Everyone is different. Figure out your own timing, and then work the week in a way that works for you.

The 80/20 Principle, in all its applications, allows you to understand who your best clients and opportunities are, how you work best, what *exactly* requires your strict attention and when you're most productive. This knowledge lets you work with focus that ultimately will translate to increased success. And when this 80/20 approach is coupled with an abundance mind-set, you'll see which of your many opportunities will best help you achieve your goals and reach your full potential. You can work with increased focus and more purpose, doing the activities and targeting the clients and opportunities that are right for you.

Rainmakers know this. But it's no secret. It's just how you Do What You Do Better.

Rainmaker Productivity Test

How do you measure up in terms of being a rainmaker? The key is not only working hard, but also working smart. Our **Rainmaker Productivity Test** is a simple but eye-opening exercise that will indicate which specific parts or activities in your business day need some extra attention and more effort. Once you know your strengths and weaknesses, in terms of working smarter, you can do what you do better.

Ready to learn? Rate yourself on 10 different activities/aspects of a typical business day using the scoring system below:

Possible score for each question:

- **10 points** if you can answer: **"always"**
- **7 points** if you can say yes: **"most days"**
- **5 points** if your answer is: **"depends on the day and week"**
- **3 points** if your answer is: **"not usually"**
- **1 point** if your answer is: **"never"**

1. Do you arrive in the office at your target time? "Target time" is defined as the time you *should* be in the office in order to make the most of your day. (For most people, 7:45 a.m. would be a good target time.)
   Score: _____
2. Do you thoroughly work through each day's To Do list, daily planner & your Best Bets™ Opportunities?
   Score: _____
3. At the end of your current workweek, do you schedule face-to-face sales calls for the next week?
   Score: _____
4. Do you limit your non-business phone calls, emails, etc. to no more than two a day during office hours? (Personal calls in the car while driving or at lunch don't count, but we don't recommend the driving ones.)
   Score: _____

5. Do you spend time every day on your "hour of power" calls? And do you schedule—and accomplish—regular follow-up with your current and future Best Bets™ Opportunities?

Score: _____

6. Are you "in your sales zone" before 9 a.m.? (Do you make at least five business-related calls by 9 or 9:30 a.m.?)

Score: _____

7. Do you stop and take time to review your To Do list, daily planner or Best Bets™ Opportunity Pipeline at least once a day so you can stay on track?

Score: _____

8. Do the co-workers or other salespeople who know you and watch your progress consider you "in the game" on a daily basis?

Score: _____

9. Do you enjoy going to work? Are you enthusiastic about your work and the selling process? (Think about this carefully, and be totally authentic with yourself before you answer this question.)

Score: _____

10. Are you able to leave the office at your targeted time? "Targeted time" is defined as the time you ideally want to leave in order to spend quality time with family or friends, or to exercise and do the things you want to do after work.

Score: _____

Now, total up your points and see where you stand.

Score: 90 - 100 Points — *Rainmaker*
Score: 80 - 89 Points — *Rainmaker Potential*
Score: 70 - 79 Points — *Above Average Performance*
Score: 60 - 69 Points — *Average Performance*
Score: 59 or Fewer Points — *Out of the Game*

An Abundance of Workable Tips (and Some Commonsense Sayings)

1. **Forget your past—there's no future in it.** The skills and habits that got you where you are today are, in many cases, not necessarily the skills you need in your future. Embrace (better yet, seek out) change. Don't be afraid to try new ways of doing what you do better.

2. **Time is a perishable resource—use it wisely.** That is why God gives it to us one second at a time. Do not waste it or take it for granted. Take control of your time.

3. ***"There is no waste of time like making explanations."*** — Benjamin Disraeli

4. **Work smarter—not harder and longer.** Remember Parkinson's Law: ***"Work expands to fill the time available for its completion."*** Accomplish (not work) as much as you can in the shortest amount of time. There's a huge difference.

5. **Prioritize.** You only have enough time in your day to do the important and urgent things. A day consists of three kinds of activities: ***Have* to do, *need* to do and *nice* to do.** Forget the nice to do's. Start with the have to do's and work your way backward. **Spend your first hour at work on your most important activity of the day.** Then pick the next most important and so on. (And don't begin your day with 30 minutes of emailing. Once you start to get return messages, it's hard to stop and move on to more important things.)

6. ***"You can gauge a person's ambition and competitiveness by whether they hate their alarm clock or consider it a resource to help them do what they do better in life."*** — Marc Corsini

7. **Delegate to others—inside and outside of the organization.** Ask yourself with every activity: *"Is there someone else who could do this better, faster, easier or cheaper (hourly cost) than I?"* Look for help inside your organization as well as outside. In the past, most people only used outside sources for things like accounting needs. Today, you can find people who, on a freelance basis, will write, produce graphic artwork, perform secretarial and IT tasks, handle your public relations and human-resource needs, run errands, manage your database and schedule appointments for you.

8. **Remember the 3Ds of delegation.** Do it, delegate it or ditch it. Work with the 80/20 Principle in mind, and don't waste time on things or activities that aren't rewarding for you. Delegate what you can, and focus your energies on what really matters.

9. *"If there is no wind, row."* — Latin proverb

10. **Do it right the first time.** Our experience shows it takes about 15 percent more time to do a job right the first time. We all know people who don't have time to do a job/task right— but they seem to have time to do the job over again. That's no way to work. It's not fair to the client or to you. Besides, doing something right the first time is consistent with the idea of being authentic in all you do.

11. **Finish what you start.** As Napoleon Hill stated, *"Most of us are great 'starters' but poor 'finishers' in everything we do."* Be the person others count on.

12. *"In the morning be first up, and in the evening last to go to bed, for they that sleep catch no fish."* — English proverb

13. **Channel your energy.** Experts used to tell us to spend one hour each day concentrating on a single important task. But few of us have an extra quiet hour in our day. Don't worry about finding and spending a quiet hour in order to complete an important task; just **concentrate on spending all your available time on a single, important task** between interruptions, phone calls and meetings.

14. **Focus on outcomes, not activities.** Nobody cares how hard you're working—nobody. They only care about what you're accomplishing.

15. *"Unless you're serving time, there's never enough of it."* — Malcolm Forbes

16. **Look for robbers.** Some people can—and will—rob you of your time. Time robbers can be anyone—co-workers, friends, vendors, family and some clients. **Avoid, ignore, put off and manage those who rob you of your time.**

17. **Learn to say "no" or "not now."** Only be overly accessible to your Best Bets™ Opportunities and clients. Learn to say "no" or "not now" to the requests of others. Agree to meet, but at a later time or date when someone requests your help tackling a problem. Most likely, they will figure out the answer by themselves before you have time to meet. This saves you time and teaches them problem-solving skills, too.

18. ***"Until you value yourself, you will not value your time. Until you value your time, you will not do anything with it."*** — M. Scott Peck

19. **"Quick questions" are never quick.** Quick questions do not mean short interruptions. Watch out for that trap.

20. **End your "pilot" program**. We all know people who have multiple "piles" on their desk. Tame the paper tiger—clear the clutter off your desk. Get rid of all those distractions. Throw it all away. File it. Just make sure you act on it in some way. Completely clear off your desk once a week or at a minimum once a month.

21. ***"Fifty percent of a salesperson's time is wasted on poor opportunities. The problem is, a lot of salespeople do not know who these useless opportunities are until after they finish the sales cycle. That's because they treat all opportunities the same."*** — Marc Corsini

22. **Give yourself margin.** Schedule margin on your calendar and in your meetings so you can handle unexpected client and Best Bets™ Opportunities activities and issues. No margin—no peace. Have margin—have peace.

23. **Make appointments with yourself.** When you have an important project you need to work on, schedule time on your calendar to complete the task. Also include time for your "hour of power" so you can consistently follow up with opportunities in your Best Bets™ Pipeline, send thank-you notes, etc.

24. ***"Time is what we want most but what we use worst."*** — William Penn

25. **What's more important than a To Do list?** It's the "stop doing" list. Think about the things you do today because you're simply used to doing them. If they don't matter anymore, stop doing them.

26. **Stop filing!** A Stanford University study found that only 13 percent of filed papers are ever looked at a second time. Maybe it's time to get rid of most of your paper files.

27. ***"Time is like money, the less we have of it to spare the farther we make it go."*** — Josh Billings

28. **Develop a sense of urgency.** The best cure for procrastination is to develop a strong sense of urgency.

29. **Be a planner.** You might be shocked to know that for every one minute of planning, you save 10 minutes in execution. Set aside the last 15 minutes of each business

day to evaluate what you have done that day and what you plan to do the next day. Establish and prioritize your objectives, to do's and appointments for the coming day. Avoid the "planning paradox" of failing to plan because it takes time. Include short- and long-term planning. **Try using Monday or Friday as the day you consider long-term planning.**

30. *"Know the true value of time; snatch, seize and enjoy every moment of it. No idleness; no laziness; no procrastination; never put off until tomorrow what you can do today."* — Lord Chesterfield

31. *"We all suffer the pain of discipline or the pain of regret."* Jim Rohn, the legendary speaker, was right. Either we can take control of our day and have the temporary pain of discipline to accomplish what's important to us, or we can experience the more lasting pain of regret for not being all we can be.

32. **Take weekly or monthly "vacations."** Many people are the most productive right before they go on a vacation. They have a heightened sense of urgency. They delegate. They focus. They work on the most important projects and forget the other stuff. **Pick one day a week (or at a minimum, a couple days a month), and work like you are about to go on vacation for a month.**

33. *"If you want to know a person's values, look at where they spend their time, money and energy."* — Unknown

34. **Leave an hour early.** Having trouble getting it all done? Plan to leave an hour early. If you're still having trouble, leave two hours early. Having less time to get things done forces people to only work on the really important tasks. By reducing the amount of time you have, **you force yourself to work on results—not merely work.**

35. **Throw out your electronic day timer.** Most people use their day timer to fill up their day, and that keeps them from really focusing on results. They include all kinds of to do's that are not helping them get to where they want to be. Use a 3-x-5 index card instead. On one side, write the three most important things you need to do that day. Use the rest of the space to make notes as people call you. On the other side, list your appointments and meetings. **Review the card at the end of the day, and decide on the three most important things you need to do the next day.**

36. ***"Time is really the only capital that any human being has, and the only thing he can't afford to lose."*** — Thomas Edison

37. **Stop playing telephone tag.** Minimize telephone tag by improving your timing and scheduling calls when you are most likely to reach someone. You also should develop additional contacts within an organization; get to know your contacts' assistants. Leave careful, creative voice mail messages defining *exactly* what you need and your time frame. Establish regular "in-office hours" so people know when they can reach you. Update your outgoing message daily to reflect changes in your schedule. And use email to better communicate. Set up your email to auto-respond to messengers when you are out of town. **Caution: Email does not deepen relationships—that requires face-to-face time.** Remember this.

38. **Simplify your life.** Simply remove those activities that take up your time and yet have low payback or do not add value to your work and personal life. Ask yourself: *"Which activities make me money? Which help my career or provide value to my family, clients or employees?"* Remove those activities that don't.

39. ***"If you want to make good use of your time, you've got to know what's most important and then give it all you've got."*** — Lee Iacocca

40. **Take time off.** Take time for yourself to dream, pray, relax, learn, exercise, nurture relationships and have fun. All work and no play will make Johnny unhappy and not a fun person to be around. Be good to yourself. **Live the life of abundance.**

A Whole-Life
Approach to Success

And now we come to the second part of this book. The previous chapters have given you plenty of solid, practical, workable ideas for making the most of your **Fundamentals of Selling**. But success in the office is just part of the picture. *True* success touches *all* areas of your life. And so we'll spend time guiding you to worthwhile, life-changing achievements in the other of our **7 F's of *True* Success**—sound **Finances** (and creating your financial legacy), being someone your **Family** (and friends) can count on, the rewarding role **Faith** can have in your life, the importance of making time for **Fitness** and **Fun** and the **Fusion** (or balance) of all this.

Each of these elements is crucial to your ultimate, *true* success, and so we devote a chapter to every one of them. Move on to the next pages, and begin to Do What You Do Better.

Finances
(and Creating Your Financial Legacy)

"Don't follow a money trail. Take charge of your finances. To get ahead and stay ahead, you must know where your money's going."

— Marc Corsini

INSIDE
10 Tips for Financial Success

We've spent several chapters discussing the **Fundamentals of Selling**. This makes sense since, together, we are working on the essential elements of your being effective and successful at work. But in keeping with a whole-life approach to your success, we should address the other factors to a life of balance. The **Fundamentals of Selling** is only the first component of **The 7 F's of *True* Success**. In the next several chapters, we'll look at the other F's—sound **Finances** (and your financial legacy), the importance of **Family** (and friends), **Faith**, **Fitness**, **Fun** and **Fusion** (the balance of all this).

We devoted an entire book to this method. ***Do What You Do Better With the 7 F's of True Success*** addresses the key common elements to any life of real success. But here's the neat part: With this book, you can easily make our **7 F's** system your own. Various chapters in this book require serious thought.

Let us first look at developing sound **Finances** and ways to create your financial legacy. Your financial goals are yours alone. How you do what you do better with them is up to you. As you read this book, you'll narrow your focus on what truly matters in your life—both in and outside the office.

We suggest after reading this book that you take time and have your finances and financial goals organized and working for you. Possible information and reports to consider compiling include:

- quarterly or annual records or knowledge of personal net worth;
- statements with your account status from financial institutions;

- insurance policies;
- an updated will;
- articles and financial newsletters with tips on creating your financial legacy.

Be creative; use your financial imagination. You'll find other tip here, too.

Let's begin by talking about your personal **Finances** and where you are in creating your financial legacy. We're not going to walk you through the mechanics of developing a budget (bu there are some tips on the following pages). We will stress tha using your money wisely and living within your means are crucia to *true* financial success, but mainly we're going to look at the bigger picture.

A long-term financial strategy not only offers you persona security and comfort, but it also can provide a lasting legacy fo your family and even your family's family. **It's pretty exciting to think about how your actions today can benefit your children's children 30 to 40 years from now.**

In order to leave a legacy, you must accomplish something sig-nificant. It takes planning, smart decisions and hard work. This sort of achievement doesn't happen overnight. It evolves ove time.

Your financial legacy could grow from something as simple as an educational savings plan for your child in which you put aside $100 each month starting the very month the child is born. If you did this—utilizing one of the many different types of educational investment programs available today—you'd have a substantial amount accumulated by the time the child is ready for college.

Or let's say you are just out of college yourself, and you decide to purchase a rental property every five years until you reach retirement age. (This might mean you defer living in a home you actually own for a period of time while your earnings and/ or savings accumulate enough to allow you to purchase your own home.) If you purchase your first rental property at age 22, by the time you are 52 you'll have seven rental investments providing you an ongoing income stream.

Both these examples start with a simple idea. They involve a series of small steps, and they evolve into a large, long-term plan.

A smart, goal-oriented financial strategy yields more than monetary results. First, **it allows you to create your financial *legacy*.** Second, **it provides your children with a model for establishing their own spending and saving habits.** You are leaving not only a legacy of wealth, but also one of knowledge about financial stewardship that could impact many generations.

For more on this topic of creating wealth, we suggest reading or listening to *Rich Dad, Poor Dad* by Robert T. Kiyosaki.

Remember, sound financial habits don't just happen. Financial legacies aren't established by chance. Financial freedom is created through planning, discipline and action. It can take a long time to become significant. But it won't happen if you don't take charge. Do something financially significant, and start today. It's part of Doing What You Do Better.

10 Tips for Financial Success

1. Get paid what you're worth and spend less than you earn.

No matter how much you're paid, you'll never get ahead if you spend more than you earn. Make sure you know what your job is worth in the marketplace. Do this by evaluating your skills, productivity, job tasks, contribution to the company, and the going rate (both inside and outside the company) for what you do. Being underpaid even a thousand dollars a year can have a significant cumulative effect over the course of your working life.

2. Create and stick to a budget.

Everyone needs a budget, whether you make tens of thousands or hundreds of thousands each year. How can you know where your money is going if you don't budget? How can you set spending and saving goals if you don't keep track of your finances? To establish a realistic budget, keep track of all your bills and write down everything you spend for several months. Then, start living with your budget by writing checks (or setting up automatic bill payment) for necessities and give yourself a cash allowance for everything else. Spend only what you have readily available each month.

3. Get rid of credit card debt.

Credit card debt is the number one obstacle to getting ahead financially. Those little pieces of plastic are so easy to use. Some cards you only have to wave over the credit-card keypad; it's like magic. And so it's easy to forget tha we're dealing with real money when we use them. Here' the reality: If you don't pay off balances quickly, you enc up paying far more for things than you would have paid i you had used cash.

4. Plan ahead for your retirement.

Create a vision for your retirement—not only how you wan to live and where, but also what you want to do. Then plar to fund your future by contributing to a retirement plan. I your employer has a 401(k) plan and you don't contribute to it, you're throwing away a great opportunity. If you're already contributing, try to increase your contribution. I your employer doesn't offer a retirement plan, consider ar IRA. On a related note: Employment benefits like flexible spending accounts, medical and dental insurance, etc. are worth big bucks. Make sure you're maximizing yours anc taking advantage of the ones that can save you money b reducing taxes or out-of-pocket expenses.

5. Have a savings plan.

Pay yourself first! Set aside a minimum of 5 percent to 10 per cent of your salary for savings before you start paying you bills. Consider having this money automatically deductec from your paycheck and deposited into a separate account If you wait until you've met all your other financial obligation: before tending to what's left over for saving, you'll probabl never have a healthy savings account or money-making investments. If you're contributing to a retirement plan anc a savings account and you can still manage to put some money into other investments, do it.

6. Do your homework.

Whatever you're planning to do—buying a home, buying a car, investing in the stock market, whatever—do some research first. Educate yourself before you take action.

7. Build an emergency fund.

Save at least three to six months of living expenses in case of job loss, health problems or family emergencies. Prepare for the unexpected.

Schedule a financial check-up.

Review your credit report annually for inaccurate information as well as signs of identity theft. Also, invest in a paper shredder at home, and use it to shred all those pre-approved credit card offers and old financial documents.

Take care of those you love.

Estate planning isn't just for those with very large estates. It's a sad truth that 70 percent of Americans don't have a will. If you have dependents, no matter how little or how much you own, you need a will. Protect your loved ones. Write a will. On a similar note: Review your insurance coverages. It's important that you have enough insurance to protect your dependents and your income in the case of death or disability.

0. Keep good records.

That budget-building exercise of keeping track of your expenses over several months can get you into this good habit. Here's the thing: If you don't keep good records, you're probably not claiming all your allowable income-tax deductions and credits. So set up a system now, and then use it all the time. You'll find that tax time is easier, too, when you don't have to scramble to find everything and risk missing items that might save you money.

Family
(and Friends)

"Strong relationships depend on loyalty, shared experiences, and simple kindness and consideration. Forging solid ties with family and friends takes some work (and time) on your part. But it's well worth your effort."

— **Marc Corsini**

INSIDE
Strengthening Family Ties
Life In a Jar

We've focused a lot of positive energy on the **Fundamentals of Selling**. And in the last chapter, we discussed the powerful (and lasting) impact you can make with your family (and your family's family) by being disciplined enough to create your **Financial** legacy.

We know that a balanced life also includes focus on the other F's—**Family**, **Faith**, **Fitness**, **Fun** and **Fusion** (the balance of all this.)

Now, let's turn our attention to **Family** (and friends).

When we talk about "family," we mean the families we're born into as well as those we create with our spouses and children and with our friends. We include this broad definition because most of us have had at least one true friend who has brought us as much joy, fulfillment and support as any family member ever could have done.

Most of us have more to do than there are hours in which to do it all. Meetings, emails, reports, appointments and more all need your attention. If you don't watch out, you'll find yourself expanding your work time beyond the traditional 50-plus hours a week, and that cuts into your family time. With today's technology, your office can be anywhere you choose to open up your laptop—at the ballpark, library, playground and at home. All these areas were traditionally considered to be family sanctuaries.

We realize that *true* success is more than having a corner office on the top floor. It's more than all the financial rewards that go with that achievement. Succeeding at work while life at home suffers might produce a large bank account, but a messy divorce can shrink that hard-earned wealth with the stroke of a pen. This doesn't even take into account the heart-wrenching costs that go with the breakup of a family.

Our whole-life approach to coaching considers happiness at home an important part of *true* success. For greater success *in* the office, you have to get to work *outside* the office. That means giving regular and undivided attention to family and friends. Work hard and smart, and know when to shut down the computer, take off the headset and turn off your portable phone. Living a life of abundance means you *can* have it all—but you have to do your homework.

Realize that little conversations, small gestures of comfort, simple things that you do every day (whether for an hour or for just a few minutes) are often enough—especially when these things are done with sincerity and commitment to building and strengthening the bonds that you have with your family and friends.

Sit back, and think about your family and friends and what they mean to you. What parts of your relationships need your attention? What is important to you all? What possible information can you keep close at hand to help you in your close relationships? We suggest this as a start:

1. A list of birthdays and anniversaries of family and friends so you can send them cards on their special occasions.
2. Pictures of your family—for sharing and for yourself.
3. Family-tree diagrams to remind you of ties near and far.
4. A running list of school and social functions.
5. Clothing and shoe sizes so your surprises will delight (and fit).

You, of course, can come up with many more. But attention to these things is more important than the length of the list. Be creative, and then act. Consider the tips beginning on the next page as you develop and strengthen your all-important family ties. And then read the inspiring story at the end of this chapter. It is simple but full of useful truth.

Focus on your family and friends every chance you get. Make those chances happen often. That's how you Do What You Do Better.

Strengthening Family Ties

1. **Make small talk.**

   Talk in the car on the way to and from school. Talk around the dinner table. You can learn a lot from small, informal conversations. These are the times when kids talk about their life in school or some incident on the play area. Often, it is in these conversations that parents find out about bullying, difficulties in school and problems with friends. Think about each member of your family. During the last week, what are the things you have talked (or yelled) about? Make a note about whether the talk was friendly (helpful, happy) or unfriendly (angry, hurtful). Make a list like this: (a) name of family member, (b) what you talked about and (c) was the talk friendly or unfriendly? This exercise will do a great deal to help you see how communication works in your family.

2. **Spend time away from the television and other technology.**

   Just turn them off, and tune into each other. Limit your screen time to just a few hours a week, and you'll be surprised how close you become. Take a trip to a state park cabin without a television, and make your own fun. (It's not as traumatic as your kids might initially think.) Don't play movies on car trips. Instead, play tried-and-true travel games like the license plate game. Make your own fun.

3. **Hug.**

   There is so much good in giving a hug. According to research, touch therapy is very effective in building family relationships—especially those bonds between parents and their children. Hugs, or other simple, friendly touches like a pat on the back, are an excellent way of expressing your love and concern. Hold hands with your spouse. Develop signals that say, "I love you." Kiss goodbye in the morning and hello every evening. That's a nice habit to have, and you can say a lot without saying a word.

4. **Leave messages.**

   Maintain communication in whatever form you choose to use. Parents can use their mobile phones to keep track of their older children through their mobile phones. Messages left on a family bulletin board or posted on the refrigerator are also great ways of maintaining your presence in your family's life. Put messages in school lunches. Hide them beneath the breakfast plates. Leave unexpected notes of praise. Put your thoughts for your family down on paper.

5. Go out on a date with your spouse.

Fun time alone together is especially important if you have children. A date also is an excellent time to share dreams with each other. Pick something both of you enjoy. Compromise. Avoid conflict of any sort on your date, and simply concentrate on enjoying your time together.

6. Treat each other with respect and kindness.

Too often we talk to our family one way and to our business acquaintances in another (more considerate) way. Strange but true. Treat each family member with the same degree of respect you have for your most valued clients. Compliment each other often. Say "thank you" for little kindnesses and "please" with any request. Showing kindness in little ways strengthens any relationship and it also keeps minor annoyances from being blown out of proportion, Daily acts of kindness also can promote the growth of romance in a marriage. Respect and care for each other in ordinary ways. You'll end up with extraordinary results.

7. Establish your own family traditions.

Traditions and rituals serve important functions in families. First, they enable us to figure out what's really important to us. They also give meaning and predictability to family life. Rituals help make special times more special and ordinary times less stressful. Studies show that relationships that are marked by numerous traditions and rituals are often richer and more purposeful than those that are not.

8. Be with them.

Despite your busy schedule, make an effort to be there for your family whenever possible. Show up at the school festival. Coach your kid's soccer team if you can; seasons aren't very long. A once-a-month family getaway can greatly strengthen family ties. This can be something as simple as a night out at the movies or as big as a weekend trip to the beach. Find common ground within the family, and learn to make compromises not only on your schedules but also on your various interests. Take turns going to your favorite places when out on a family trip. Better yet, let a different family member plan each outing from start to finish.

9. Celebrate special occasions.

School presentations and sporting events are big things in the life of a child. Sharing them as a family strengthens your bonds. It is important that you support your children in their various projects. Also, take the initiative when planning a birthday or anniversary celebration. Make the reservations. Hire the sitter. All this shows your family that they matter to you and that you are willing and happy to give them a portion of your very valuable time.

10. Recipe for a happy marriage:

Combine two **caring hearts**. Melt into one. Add a lot of **love**. Mix well with **respect** and **trust**. Add **gentleness**, **laughter**, **faith**, **hope** and **joy**. Pour in much **understanding** (and a lot of **patience**). Sprinkle with **kisses** and a dash of **hugs**. Bake for a **lifetime**. Yield: **One Happy Couple**.
— Author unknown

Sure it's cute, but it's also true. Even if you can't cook, you can make this happen.

Life In a Jar

When things in your life seem too much to handle, when 24 hours in a day are just not enough, think about this life lesson from a very smart teacher:

A professor stood before his philosophy class with some items in front of him. When the class began, he wordlessly picked up a very large and empty jar and proceeded to fill it with golf balls. He then asked the students if the jar was full. They agreed that it was.

The professor then picked up a handful of pebbles and poured them into the jar. He shook the jar lightly, and the pebbles rolled into the open areas between the golf balls. He then asked the students again if the jar was full. They agreed it was.

Next, the professor picked up a box of sand and poured it into the jar. Of course, the sand filled up every other space. He asked once more if the jar was full. The students responded with an enthusiastic "yes."

The professor then set two cups of coffee on his table. Then he poured both cups into the jar, effectively filling the empty space between the sand. The students laughed.

"Now," said the professor, as the laughter subsided, "I want you to recognize that this jar represents your life. The golf balls are the important things—your family, your children, your health, your friends and your favorite passions—and if everything else were lost and only they remained, your life would still be full.

"The pebbles are the other things that matter like your job, your house and your car. The sand is everything else—the small stuff. If you put the sand into the jar first," he continued, "there is no room for the pebbles or the golf balls. The same goes for life. If you spend all your time and energy on the small stuff, you will never have room for the things that are truly important to you."

He told them: "Pay attention to the things that are critical to your happiness. Play with your children. Take time to get medical checkups. Take your spouse out to dinner. Play another 18 holes. There will always be time to clean the house and fix the disposal. Take care of the golf balls first—the things that really matter. Set your priorities. The rest is just sand."

One of the students raised her hand then and asked what the coffee represented.

The professor smiled. "I'm glad you asked," he said. "It just goes to show you that no matter how full your life might seem, there's always room for a couple cups of coffee with a friend."

— Author unknown

Faith

"Faith provides guiding principles to help you make decisions in life—in and out of the office. Follow your faith's principles, and you won't go wrong."

— Marc Corsini

INSIDE

Talking About Faith

While this book mainly is about the **Fundamentals of Selling**, that is just the first component of the larger, **7 F's of *True* Success** method of achieving a balanced life. We've talked about the benefits of sound **Finances** and having a financial legacy. We've addressed the importance of **Family** (and friends). Now let's look at **Faith**—in and outside the workplace.

Operating with faith in a business environment can be tricky at times. Let's face it; you might risk making some people uncomfortable. Of course, there are much worse things than that, but you do want to be respectful of others. We've found in this hustle-bustle world, now more than ever, people want work that fits in with a larger sense of purpose in life. Working with a spiritual attitude can make this happen.

At some time or another, all devoted people struggle with integrating faith and work. Most of us know exactly how to be religious out of the office and how to be successful at work. But sometimes it's hard to know how to do both at the same time.

You've probably heard the saying, *"God on Sunday; and by God, watch out on Monday."*

We all realize this is not the way it should be. To be truly happy in your life (and not torn by conflict), you have to "walk the talk" of your faith. If you truly believe in your faith, it's a 24-7-365 proposition. If you act one way on your weekly holy day and differently the other six days of the week, there's no way you can ever be authentic with yourself or anyone else.

We have an uncomplicated solution: When faced with some hard choices—in or out of the office—ask yourself three simple questions to see if your planned course of action passes a moral litmus test and aligns with your faith's beliefs:

Would my parents be proud of me?

Would my spouse respect me?

Would my children look up to me?

And the final test, of course, would be to ask yourself: **Would God approve of me?**

Now, think about your faith and what's important to you spiritually on a day-to-day basis. As you reflect on your spiritual life, what do you want to keep track of? What things can help you walk the talk at work? Perhaps you want to pray about it. Then come up with some daily reminders of your faith. Some possible things you might consider are:

- a prayer list;
- religious sayings;
- spiritual notes;
- religious books;
- a calendar marking religious celebrations (familiar and obscure).

Know your faith's commandments, and follow them. Your faith will keep you grounded and guide you to do the right thing. Use your "spiritual muscles" daily. That is a sure way to Do What You Do Better.

Talking About Faith

"I tell you the truth, if you have faith as small as a mustard seed, you can say to this mountain, 'Move from here to there' and it will move. Nothing will be impossible for you."
— Matthew 17:20

We think this verse speaks to the power of faith as it relates to the workplace, no matter what the job. You sometimes might feel like you are called upon to move mountains. Have faith, and work with faith. Do that, and you can work wonders.

Here are a few smart, inspirational sayings that also apply to faith in the workplace:

- Dear God, I have a problem. It's me.
- Growing old is inevitable. Growing UP is optional.
- There is no key to happiness. The door is always open.
- Silence is often misinterpreted but never misquoted.
- Do the math; count your blessings.

- Faith is the ability to not panic.
- Laugh every day, it's like inner jogging.
- If you worry, you didn't pray. If you pray, don't worry.
- As a child of God, prayer is kind of like calling home every day.
- Blessed are the flexible for they shall not be bent out of shape.
- The most important things in your house are the people.
- When you get tangled up in your problems, be still. God wants us to be still so He can untangle the knot.
- A grudge is a heavy thing to carry.

Here are some Bible verses, quotes and faith-related notes we've taken over the years. Get in the habit of jotting down inspirational conversations or just snippets of conversations. Carry a favorite Bible verse with you in your wallet. These are acts of faith with immediate and long-term rewards.

- Why did God create us? To know Him, love Him and to serve Him.
- Don't try to impress people with what you have; instead, impress them with your life.
- *"Hail Mary, full of grace; help us find a parking place."* — uttered by a 3-year-old child
- We sometimes buy things that we do not want in order to impress people that we do not like.
- Christ didn't promise you a smooth road in life; He promised to walk that road with you.
- God Answers Knee Mail — seen on a bumper sticker
- *"A priest's job is to comfort the afflicted and affect the comfortable."* — spoken during a sermon
- *"You can catch more flies with honey than with vinegar."* — St. Francis de Sales
- *"Vice hurts, virtue heals."* — Father Jim Hedderman
- There is hope for the hopeless.
- *"In thinking of death, I can't wait to meet Jesus."* — Monsignor Martin Muller repeating a statement a lady told him
- Mother Angelica's definition of faith: *"One foot on the ground, one foot in the air and a queasy feeling in your stomach."*

- When we pray to God for something, God gives us one of three answers:
  1. Yes.
  2. Not yet.
  3. I have a better way.
- *"An attitude of gratitude leads to the Beatitudes."*
  — Father Jim Hedderman
- *"In life, there is more inspiration than temptation."*
  — Father Jim Hedderman
- St. Anthony of Lost Items revised prayer:
  "Tony, Tony come around; something's lost and needs to be found."
  — spoken by a priest during his sermon
- *"No prophet is accepted in his own country."* — Luke 4:24
- Five Stages of Dying:
  1. Denial.
  2. Anger.
  3. Bargaining.
  4. Depression.
  5. Acceptance of God's will.
- *"God must have loved beauty because he made so much of it."* — repeated by Monsignor Martin Muller after a comment made to him

Fitness

*"Being fit—emotionally and physically—is crucial
to achieving your 'everything.'"*

— Marc Corsini

INSIDE

Success in Motion

Healthy Thoughts: 10 Ways to De-Stress

You might be wondering why a *business* coach would make such a big deal out of **Fitness**. That's because we recognize that good health—*emotional* as well as *physical*—is necessary for a life of *true* success. When you are emotionally and physically fit, you are more able to achieve your goals and you're in a better position to enjoy them.

Fitness is one of **The 7 F's of *True* Success** in our approach to a balanced life. We've devoted many chapters of this book to the **Fundamentals of Selling**. We looked at the impact you can have on your family and your family's family by being disciplined with your **Finances** and creating your financial legacy. We focused on the importance of **Family** (and friends), and we've discussed the power of leading and working each day with **Faith**.

So let's continue to be faithful to our whole-life approach, and look at how to make physical and mental fitness two of your greatest strengths.

There's an Arabian proverb that goes like this: *"He who has health has hope; he who has hope has everything."*

Emotional and physical fitness take into account mind, body and spirit. It's about feeling good and feeling good about you. This frame of mind influences so many things: your work, finances, family relationships, your spiritual life and your ability to enjoy all that life has to offer. Fitness is absolutely key to achieving success through the **7 F's**.

Think about your levels of physical and emotional fitness. Are you happy with how you look and feel? Are you happy period?

You should know that even people who are thin need to think about physical exercise because of the benefits to their body.

Some of the items that can help you get fit (and stay on track) include the following:

- an exercise chart;
- results of your latest physical checkup;
- articles on reducing stress in the office;
- a steady supply of good books;
- maps of local walking and biking trails.

The American College of Sports Medicine and the Centers for Disease Control and Prevention have published national guidelines on physical activity. According to these guidelines, all healthy adults aged 18 to 65 need moderate-intensity aerobic (endurance) physical activity for a minimum of 30 minutes five days a week or vigorous-intensity aerobic physical activity for a minimum of 20 minutes three days each week.

Breaking up your activities into short bursts, such as two 15-minute sessions in a day, has about the same benefits as one 30-minute session. Combinations of moderate- and vigorous-intensity activity also will meet this recommendation. For example, a person might walk briskly for 30 minutes twice during the week and then jog for 20 minutes on three other days. Moderate-intensity activity, which is generally equivalent to a brisk walk and noticeably accelerates the heart rate, can be done in several bouts each lasting 10 or more minutes. Know that moderate physical activity includes things like walking up a few flights of stairs, mowing the lawn, washing the car, vacuuming the house. It's mainly about moving.

In addition, every adult should perform activities that maintain or increase muscular strength and endurance. This should be done a minimum of two days each week. Activities like yoga or Pilates or weight training will take care of this.

You'll want to make fitness a priority in your life. Get moving, and get fit. But don't stop there. Use the abundance principle to take a mind, body and spiritual approach to fitness. Look for ways to decrease your stress. Laugh. Take time just for you. You'll work smarter, and you'll Do What You Do Better.

Success in Motion

Whether it is a structured exercise program or just part of your daily routine, all exercise adds up to a healthier you. Here are some tips for exercise success:

- Exercise should be fun, not exhausting. Add variety. Develop a repertoire of several activities that you can enjoy. That way, exercise will never seem boring or routine.
- Wear properly fitted footwear and comfortable, loose-fitting clothing appropriate for the weather and the activity.
- Find a convenient time and place to do activities. Make exercise a habit, but be flexible. If you miss an exercise opportunity, work activity into your day another way. Don't beat yourself up or get sidetracked from your fitness goals.
- Use music to keep you entertained while you work out.
- Surround yourself with people who can give you the support you need. Do you want them to remind you to exercise? Ask about your progress? Participate with you regularly or occasionally? Allow you time to exercise by yourself? Go with you to a special event, such as a 10K walk/run? Spend time with your children while you exercise? Tell your support people what you need to succeed. Then consider sharing your activity time with others. Make a date with a family member, friend or co-worker. Be an active role model for your children.
- Don't overdo it. Do low- to moderate-level activities, especially at first. You can slowly increase the duration and intensity of your activities as you become more fit. Over time, work up to exercising on most days of the week for 30 to 60 minutes.
- Keep a record of your activities. Reward yourself at special milestones. Nothing motivates like success (or a new exercise outfit)!
- If you've been sedentary for a while, are overweight, have a high risk of heart disease or some other chronic health problem, see your doctor for a medical evaluation before beginning a physical activity program.

Healthy Thoughts: 10 Ways to De-Stress

There are many things you can do to promote emotional well-being and restore a sense of control in your life. Here are some tips for coping with job-related and general life-related stress:

1. **Write it down.**

   Make a list of the stressful factors in your life, and then brainstorm for ways to cope with each of them. Recognize those things you can change, and then change them. Deal with the rest with healthy coping skills like exercise, talking with friends, reading for pleasure and listening to music. (You'll want to practice these coping skills every day, even when you're not stressed. They'll help keep you from becoming overwhelmed, and you'll know what to do if you are.)

2. **Think happy.**

   Maintain a positive attitude. In addition to simply making you feel good, this can nurture self-confidence, which can empower you to better deal with problems. Along these same lines, avoid self-criticism, and be proud of your accomplishments no matter how big or small.

3. **Seek a workable balance.**

   Each day, seek a balance between your work and personal time. Achieving this balance is very important. If you are constantly focused on work, you'll have little time or energy to spend with family and friends. Plus, you risk job burnout.

4. **Relax.**

   Practice relaxation techniques, such as biofeedback, massage therapy; meditation or yoga. These can help reduce stress and alleviate anxiety; insomnia; depression; and physical manifestations of stress, including high blood pressure and headaches.

5. **Take a break.**

   Do something you enjoy. Go for a walk. Meet friends for coffee or lunch. Take a weekend trip with your family. Step out of your routine for a while, and let yourself regroup.

6. **Don't just sit there.**

   According to many psychologists, motion creates emotion. You might notice that when you are idle, it's easier to become depressed. Your heart rate slows down, and less oxygen travels to your brain. Get up, get out and get moving.

7. **Be in good company.**

   Call your friends, and share your problems. The wisdom of a crowd is always better than the wisdom of one. Ask for their advice or input. While their suggestions might or might not be helpful, often just talking about your issues will make you feel less stressed.

8. **Help others cope.**

   Be there for your friends. Helping others with their problems can be extremely therapeutic. You will be surprised how many people's problems are worse than those you might be facing. There are many charitable organizations that can use your help right now.

9. **Laugh.**

   Turns out that laughter *is* good medicine. It relieves tension and loosens muscles. It causes blood to flow to the heart and brain. More importantly, laughter releases a chemical that helps rid the body of pains and depressed feelings. Strive to laugh (and laugh hard) every day.

10. **Wear out your knees.**

    Pray. Take your problems to a higher power. Your faith can see you through many a stressful time.

Fun

"You have to love what you do. You spend more time working than at any other single activity in your life."
— **Marc Corsini**

INSIDE
Fun at Work
A Lesson on Stress

This is a business book for busy, effective professionals, but, seriously, we should have some **Fun** with it.

Fun happens to be one of **The 7 F's of *True* Success,** and it is just as important as the **Fundamentals of Selling;** sound **Finances** (and creating your financial legacy); being someone your **Family** (and friends) can count on; living a life of **Faith** in and out of the office; and the coming together, or **Fusion,** of all these elements. If we're to be authentic here, we need to stress the importance of having **Fun.**

Now, we're not talking about the giggly kind of fun, but rather we're referring to smart fun that works in a business setting and also to the relaxing kind of fun that brings *true* joy to you. Having fun at work is just as important as setting aside time for diversions, hobbies and recreation. We believe **you have to find joy in your work.** You spend the majority of your waking hours doing it. Here's a relevant quote that is just true enough and funny enough to resonate: *"Son, you might as well enjoy what you do because you are going to do a hell of a lot of it."* That bit of homegrown wisdom is from a man who owns a very successful construction company.

In this chapter, we're going to explore what brings you joy in your life. This is a deeper concept than it might first appear. Often people confuse the emotional ideas of "juice" and "joy." In our coaching sessions we generally ask the participants, *"What brings you joy?"* And then we usually hear about what brings them a rush of excitement or the exhilarating feeling of winning. That's "juice," not real joy.

We want you to think for a moment about what gives you a feeling of *true* joy. Whatever it is, that's the kind of fun we're talking about. It's not necessarily the rush of being named #1 in your industry by a local business journal or winning a large sought-after account. It goes deeper than that. Having fun and finding joy in what you do positively impacts all the other important aspects of your life—in a big way.

It's all connected in our whole-life approach to success. Real fun—fun with a lasting impact—brings you a deep, undeniable sense of satisfaction and happiness. We're talking about things like mentoring a co-worker, attending your book group, singing in the church choir, playing football with your kids. Notice that these are examples of fun that happen in a lot of different places—at work, with friends, at your place of worship and at home with family.

Figure out exactly how fun fits into your life with this exercise: Looking back over the past five years, what were the three to five things you did each year that were absolutely enjoyable? Chances are, some of these fun things are recurring. Good for you! Now look at your list, and see if it's balanced. Are you having fun in the various areas covered in our **7 F's** approach to success? Each aspect is important. You should be doing something you love in relation to all of them.

We want you to take some meaningful time and reflect on where the fun comes from in your life. Gather things that remind you of these fun times. You might include:

- photos of your family during vacation,
- an art project from your child,
- a love letter from your spouse,
- a birthday card from a friend,
- a favorite Bible verse.

It's really up to you. Only *you* know what truly brings you joy. Pinpoint those things, and then strive to do them more often. That's how you Do What You Do Better.

Fun at Work

Work doesn't necessarily have to be work. You should truly enjoy what you do. If you don't, you'll be stressed, anxious and downright exhausted by the end of each day.

The rainmakers we've coached who love what they do are incredibly positive people. And what's more, their **positive attitudes rub off on everyone around them**. Positive people accomplish things. People want to help them. Employees want to follow them. Employers want to reward them.

Here are just a few of the reasons why fun at work is so very important:

- Employers can better keep their most talented people happy (and content to stay put) by creating an exciting atmosphere where employees *want* to come to work. The intentional use of fun and play on the job is a great way to create an enthusiastic and committed workforce.

- Happy and healthy employees are more creative, more productive, get along better with co-workers, are better at customer service, and have greater corporate loyalty and a healthier work/life balance.

- An atmosphere of fun at work, in any organization, facilitates flexibility; change; and better communication.

The best type of fun for the workplace is playful fun—competitive or noncompetitive—that generates congratulations and cheers from co-workers. Sporting or performance types of fun fit well within the workplace where employers generally want employees to be goal-orientated and to have energy, drive, talent, determination and a competitive spirit.

In a lot of cases, the employees, not management, should generate fun at work. Otherwise, it seems dictated, and that's never much fun. Management should simply not get in the way of an appropriately fun time.

Here are some ideas for bringing a little joy to the workplace:

- Celebrate any success—no matter how big or how small—with an enthusiastic fist-in-the-air "YEESSS!" Do this regardless of the size or importance of the success. Maybe you finally finished a report, or you brought in Aunt Edna's famous brownies for everyone. It doesn't matter; celebrate.

- Bring in a bouquet of flowers, a pretty plant or an impressive trophy and present it to one of your co-workers. Say, *"I want you to keep this on your desk for the next half-hour, and then pass it on to someone else and tell them to do the same."*

- Hold a lottery where the winner gets driven to and from work in a limousine.

- Employees can enjoy a day off at the spa (they can draw for various services), or arrange a fishing trip with a BASS pro. Go to a nearby amusement park, or get outside on a nature hike and end with a picnic. The possibilities are endless.
- Have a drawing once a month for some unusual gifts (like free housecleaning certificates or a catered weeknight dinner).
- Hire an on-site massage therapist for the day.
- Ask your minister or rabbi over for lunch, or invite your vendors to your potluck. Then guess who made what, with all the dishes set anonymously on the table. Have everyone bring a dish with a personal story behind it—an ethnic specialty, a family favorite, a special dish from a local restaurant—and then share these stories.
- Invite a local chef to your company for a lunchtime demonstration / lecture about "fast meals for busy professionals."

Any of these activities will get you and your team out of your usual routine. You'll find that you and your colleagues interact with each other in an entirely new way. You'll connect, and you'll do it with energy, creativity and laughter.

So get ready, get set and have fun.

A Lesson on Stress

A lecturer, when explaining stress management to an audience, raised a glass of water and asked, "How heavy is this?"

Answers called out ranged from just a few ounces to 16 ounces.

The lecturer replied, "The absolute weight doesn't matter. It depends on how long I try to hold it. If I hold it for a minute, that's not a problem. If I hold it for an hour, I'll have an ache in my right arm. If I hold it for a day, you'll have to call an ambulance. In each case, it's the same weight, but the longer I hold it, the heavier it becomes."

He continued, "And that's the way it is with stress management. If we carry our burdens all the time, sooner or later, as the burden becomes increasingly heavy, we won't be able to carry on."

"As with the glass of water, you have to put it down for a while and rest before holding it again. When we're refreshed, we can carry on with the burden. So, before you return home tonight, put down whatever burden you've carried today. Don't carry it home. You can pick it up tomorrow."

He concluded by saying: "Let's go ahead and give this a try. Whatever burdens you're carrying now, put them down for a moment if you can. Relax; pick them up later after you've rested. Enjoy your life."

— **Author unknown**

Fusion

"True success comes from having balance in all areas of your life. It's healthy, it makes you happy, and it's how you Do What You Do Better."

— Marc Corsini

INSIDE

Balancing Act

Fusion is the happy culmination of your work with all of the first six of our **7 F's of *True* Success**. **Fusion** is what happens when you focus on, and successfully integrate, the **Fundamentals of Selling** with smart **Finances**; attention to **Family** (and friends); a life of **Faith;** enough time to work on your physical and mental **Fitness;** and a real sense of **Fun**—in and out of your office.

In the whole-person approach we advocate in this book, fusion is absolutely necessary if you're to be truly successful.

A recent study of more than 50,000 employees from a variety of manufacturing and service organizations found that two out of every five of these employees were dissatisfied with the balance between their work and their personal lives. What causes this lack of balance? It's due to long work hours, changing demographics, more time spent in the car just to get to and from work, the deterioration of boundaries between work and home, and increased work pressure, just to name a few things. The average workweek is now around 46 hours for most Americans. You might find yourself working even more than that.

Sometimes this can't be avoided, but if you find yourself neglecting other important areas of your life such as family, friends, your spiritual time and your fun pursuits in favor of work-related goals, that's a problem.

Bottom line: A life of balance is a successful life of significant happiness. And this is most definitely within your reach. Our article, **Balancing Act**, in this chapter, will get you started with 10 targeted tips on achieving a workable balance in your life.

You might also consider some reminders of the importance of a balanced life and ideas to help you achieve it. Consider things like:

- a current schedule of the classes at a nearby fitness center,
- a list of classic books you've never read or listened to,
- alternate routes to work to circumvent traffic tie-ups,
- inspirational spiritual messages,
- photos of those you love the most.

Just considering a short list like this, there's no denying that fusion means balancing a lot of things. And because there are only so many hours in each day, this takes intensive planning and finesse. You have to work to find balance, and then it takes continued effort to maintain it.

But it's worth every effort. When you're happily doing well both in and out of your office, you'll know the meaning of *true* success. You'll know how to Do What You Do Better.

Balancing Act

Here are 10 tips to help you achieve a better balance in your life. Read, reflect, and then act. A life of balance is an ongoing process. It's also a reachable goal.

1.   Figure out what really matters.

Getting your priorities clear is the first and most essential step toward achieving a well-balanced life. Figure out what you want your priorities to be—not what you think they should be. Try this simple exercise, and ask yourself these questions:

- "If I could only focus on one thing in my life, what would that be?"
- "If I could add a second thing, what would I add?"
- "If I could add a third thing, what would that be?"
- "What if I could add a fourth?"
- "A fifth?"

If you answered authentically, you'll have a list of your top five priorities. Resolve to focus your efforts on success in these areas. Be present while you're doing this. When you're at work, concentrate on work. When you're with your family, really be there.

2.   Bow out gracefully.

Once you decide what really matters to you, drop those activities that have no place on your list of priorities. You might be devoting too much time to activities that are causing you more problems than you realized. Adjust your schedule—professional and personal—accordingly.

3.   Do what you do differently.

Progressive employers recognize the value of good employees. Many of them are quite willing to help valued employees deal with changes (both short-term or permanent) due to personal situations. Flextime, job-sharing, telecommuting or part-time employment might be viable options. If the need arises, approach this situation with a plan that shows how you will be an even more valuable and productive employee if you can modify your current work situation.

4.   Change jobs.

Some jobs are simply more stressful than others. If you're unable to find a workable balance doing what you do today, maybe you should find a less-demanding job within your chosen career. Maybe you can identify a new position with your current employer. Maybe you need to do a full-on job search. Think about it.

5.   Protect your private time.

How much do you value your personal time? You make every effort not to miss meetings or a parent-teacher conference. What about your time at the gym? Or coffee with a friend? Your private time deserves the same respect as work and appointments. Set aside time for yourself, and guard it carefully. Work your schedule around your exercise class. Take time for a real lunch away from your desk. Stop checking your phone and email messages so often. Create boundaries that keep work from intruding on personal time. Until you get into the habit of taking time for yourself, set aside space in your planner for relaxation and fun. Plan what you're going to do, and make any necessary arrangements to ensure you'll be able to keep your commitment to yourself. Take those steps; you'll be glad you did. And your family will be glad, too.

6. Slow down, and take time to enjoy your life.

Truth is, life is simply too short not to pay attention to all of it. Enjoy the things and people around you. Schedule more time between meetings. Don't make plans for every evening or weekend. Schedule (go ahead and write it down) quiet time or time for entertainment with family and friends. Find some ways to distance yourself from the things that are causing you stress.

7. Don't procrastinate.

It's pretty simple and, of course, easier said than done. But make every effort to better manage your time. For many people, most of the stress they feel comes from simply being disorganized and procrastinating and then struggling to complete tasks on time. Learn to set realistic goals and deadlines, and then stick to them. You'll work smarter and better.

8. Share your load.

Chances are, you are not the only one capable of doing most of the things you do each day. Delegate at work and at home. Can someone else write the report that you need only to then approve? Do you have to be present at all the meetings, or can you rely on a quick, succinct update? Ask family members to help you with your personal/family responsibilities. Take turns making dinner. If you cook, have someone else clean up. That can be a new rule. Taking care of the household, children or parents should not be the responsibility of just one person. Outsource whenever possible. If you are feeling overwhelmed with your family responsibilities, hire help. Most of the time, for most of your problems, there are options. You just have to find them and then act.

9. Stick to a schedule.

A schedule will help keep your boundaries clear. Figure out a weekly schedule that will accommodate your work, your family and your individual interests. A set routine makes it easier to stop thinking about work while you're home. It helps organize your time and your mind.

10. Simplify.

We all take on too many tasks and responsibilities. We try to do too much and also to own too much. Perhaps it's habit. Maybe it's human nature. Stop. Simplify your life. Change your lifestyle. Learn to say "no." Get rid of the clutter and baggage at work, at home and in your life.

Fusion, or balance in life, isn't easy. But it is very possible. And it's necessary if you are going to truly Do What You Do Better.

The Corsini Challenge

At the beginning of this book, we challenged you to be authentic with yourself and to strive to *fully* embrace the Corsini concepts. We know this to be true: If you follow these principles with focus and intent and truly understand *how* and *why* they matter to your own life, your life will be a more successful one—in and out of your office.

We went into great detail about the **Fundamentals of Selling** to achieve rainmaker status. We looked at the importance of several sales basics such as creating winning presentations, acquiring profitable references and conducting successful negotiations. We explained our Best Bets™ Model and how you can put it to work straight away—to achieve immediate results.

And we encouraged you to seek out success in *all* areas of your life. We spent several chapters emphasizing the importance of the other components of **The 7 F's of *True* Success**—sound **Finances** (and creating your financial legacy); being someone your **Family** (and friends) can count on; making time for **Faith, Fitness** and **Fun**; and the **Fusion** (or balance) of all this. When you approach the idea of success in this big-picture way, you become a rainmaker not only through your sales accomplishments at work, but also at home and in your community.

But as we've said before, all the how-tos in the world won't make that happen unless you take charge. Our whole-life approach to business coaching works. You can make it work for you. That's how you Do What You Do Better.

NOTES

NOTES

NOTES